EDGE OF THE EARTH

Stories and Images from the Antipodes

EDGE OF THE EARTH

Stories and Images from the Antipodes

VINCENT WARD

WITH ALISON CARTER, GEOFF CHAPPLE AND LOUIS NOWRA

PHOTOGRAPHS BY GEOFFREY SHORT AND MILES HARGEST

FOREWORD BY JOHN BOORMAN

HEINEMANN REED

*We are grateful to the Waimana
and Tuhoe tribal councils for their
support of this work.*

Published by Heinemann Reed, a division of Octopus
Publishing Group (NZ) Ltd, 39 Rawene Road, Birkenhead,
Auckland. Associated companies, branches and
representatives throughout the world.

ISBN 0 7900 0146 2
© 1990 Vincent Ward
First published 1990

Written with the financial assistance of the New Zealand
and Australian Film Commissions

Photographs printed by Paradise Colour in association with
Real Pictures Photographic Gallery, Auckland

Designed by Debeer Adams Associates, Auckland

Printed in Singapore

FOR TE PUHI

I have never met Vincent Ward, but his films are eerily familiar, unnervingly so. They seem to have sprung uninvited from a suppressed region of my own unconscious. It is not just the mythic dimension. It is the compositions and rhythms and structures, and most of all in the dreamscapes of his imagination, the images he conjures out of my mind.

When I was in Australia some years back Bruce Beresford took me to dinner at a place on Bondi Beach. He wanted me to see the ageing belly-dancer who performed there. He was persuaded that she was the finest exponent of the art. I was on my way to New Zealand and asked his view of it. 'If it wasn't for New Zealand,' he explained, 'Australia would be the most boring country in the world.' And I found it to be so in one sense — a population dedicated to re-enacting a parody of lost Englishness. But then I fell among the Maori, and saw how patiently and implacably they are set on subverting the sleep-walkers from London and Tunbridge Wells. I have travelled the South Seas, island by island, and know something of those peoples, particularly the Palauans on whose archipelago I committed *Hell in the Pacific*. Through them I understood that New Zealand, try as it will to masquerade as a nation, a proper country, is simply a Pacific island, the very last, most perfect island, the end of the line, the edge of the earth. The Pacific Islanders were great navigators, and they migrated compulsively. This is the furthest point, where only the bravest came.

This book is about Vincent Ward's journey to the end of the earth to make three films, and it is brave and foolhardy, like the Pacific navigators. He, like I, connected at an early point to primal, tribal people and was touched by their magic, entered their dream, and will never wholly return to his own time.

His film, *The Navigator*, is about digging a hole in medieval England and arriving in modern New Zealand. Has not every child dug specially deep in the sand of an English beach and felt the dread of falling into New Zealand? It is a mesmerising film, dredging up racial nightmares, demonstrating how the imagination squirms when it is pinioned by death.

I know from *Excalibur* how hard it is to achieve a convincing medieval milieu. Vincent Ward succeeds in expunging any trace of the modern from his players in a way that I never could. His skill is consummate, but more importantly he is that rare monster, an artist with a remorseless vision that drives him into impossible places of folly and madness.

The only worthwhile purpose of cinema now is to connect to that past, lost magic, and carry it into the future. It is painful but important. Why else would Ward suffer the tribulations he records in his memoir, sorrows so reminiscent of my own?

I say this to him: now you have included and enveloped us in your dreams you are no longer free. We oblige you to go on, and further and deeper, whatever the cost.

Fraternally from the far side of the earth, greetings.

JOHN BOORMAN

These stories are about three films and the journeys that led to their making. *Edge of the Earth* stumbled into existence over several years. I had some photographs shot on location which I felt were too good to lie wasting away in boxes. Looking at them, it struck me that hidden behind the images were other, truer stories that said more about the place and the people I come from.

ACKNOWLEDGMENTS

This book, like film-making, became a process of collaborations. It was realised with the help of many people.

WRITERS: Alison Carter helped pull together the different fragments of my story and, with Louis Nowra, we reworked the general text. *The Navigator* screenplay was translated by Geoff Chapple into a medieval codex.

EDITORS: Text was pre-edited by Helen Stanwix and Dimity Torbett before our book finally found its publisher and a very supportive editor in Chris Price. Janet Cook polished and coordinated the many changes along the way.

PHOTOGRAPHS: Miles Hargest took the location stills in Part I ('In Spring One Plants Alone') and Part II ('Making *Vigil*'). Geoffrey Short took the location stills in Part III ('The Monk's Codex'). Geoffrey Short printed the images from all three films, including those of Miles Hargest, at Real Pictures.

PRODUCTION & DESIGN: The book was designed by Mark Adams and Vincent Ward, while Julie Green, Laura Dalrymple, Sandra Collins and Susan Shehadie all assisted with visual research and layout; Marsha Bennett searched copyright and obtained clearances.

RESEARCH: My thanks for their input and advice to Steve Upston, Alun Bollinger, Anne Martin, Fiona Kay, Niki Takao, Hone Edwards, and the many members of *The Navigator* cast and crew we interviewed; to Puhi Rangiaho and Wharehuia Milroy, who checked the Maori textual references; and to my parents Pat and Judy Ward, who remained tirelessly open to my prying questions.

Special thanks to John Maynard, Graeme Tetley, Cathy Robinson, Viccy Harper, Debra Lancaster, Cathy Lovell, Charles Merriweather, and Miro Bilbrough; and to the Tuhoe elders Tawhao Tioke, Wharehuia Milroy, Hirini Melbourne, Timoti Karetu and Tommy Takao, all of whom gave so generously of their time.

Produced with the assistance of the Australian Film Commission, the New Zealand Film Commission, Real Pictures Photographic Gallery and Debeer Adams Associates, Auckland.

Part I

IN SPRING ONE PLANTS ALONE

In the valley they say it always rains when a stranger comes. It wasn't my first visit to this valley where the prophet Rua's descendants had found sanctuary, yet still it rained on me.

When the outlawed leader Te Kooti, charismatic founder of the Ringatu faith, fled to these mountains in the early 1870s, he brought down an army in pursuit that razed the Tuhoe villages and burned their crops, leaving the survivors to starve. No one had forgotten the land stolen and despoiled. A hundred years later the community at Matahi still kept to the old ways and had little to do with the Pakeha (Europeans). If there was sickness they had their own cures, and those who were mentally ill were looked after within the family. While the young men found a living through forestry and deerhunting, the old people's day-to-day lives went on as they always had, with funerals, bring-and-buys to raise funds, constant discussions and seemingly endless preparation of food — everything done to ensure that what had been passed on to them would be there for the generations to come.

Puhi sat in the back of my van, a scarf covering her head, her lips moving silently as she muttered her ancient prayers. We had just attended a funeral where the old lady had been one of the callers, the women who cry out to the ancestors and summon mourners onto the marae (meeting ground). Now as she crouched on the floor in the back of my van, she broke occasionally into a low keening, pausing to brush her eyes with her hands.

It was dusk, the sky heavy with rain. The gravel road was pitted with shining puddles.

Dripping ferns hung from the banks, their fronds scraping the windscreen as we passed. Every few miles the road emerged into a tiny clearing where the scrubby land was dominated by a wooden meeting house. There were nine guarding the valley, their lintels carved with ancestral faces, the staring eyes glittering with paua shell, the tongues outthrust.

We rounded a bend and before us, down on one knee, a man in a bush-jacket fired his .303 after a disappearing deer. In the narrow corridor of hills each blast echoed like thunder. Two frightened white horses drifted by, luminous in our headlights, then the bush closed around us again.

Through the branches a house light flickered, and seemed to be moving towards us. Then out of the blackness a massive figure loomed. Torchlight swinging, Niki had come to meet us.

This was heartland for the Tuhoe people, the Children of the Mist. I was 22, a Pakeha, I couldn't speak their language and I didn't know the codes they lived by.

I had just come out of three years at art school and I was a volatile mixture of cockiness, self-doubt, naïvety and enthusiasm. Dressing like a ragged leftover from the sixties, I had embraced the earnest belief that artists should focus on their work with religious intensity — to the extent that rather than waste time cooking, I lived on saveloys for a year. When I could no longer stand the sight of them, my obsession finally wavered.

Early in 1978 I'd been given leave to go up north, after accidentally putting my foot through my lecturer's office ceiling. He was showered with plaster and old film as he sat below enjoying a furtive snack at his desk. I imagine he identifed the protruding member by its size (big feet are in fact a family trait) and I'm sure he decided then and there that the sooner he got rid of me the better. He hauled me in and, stressing the first two words, said 'Go away, make your film'. I was happy to oblige.

It gave me the opportunity to travel to Te Urewera (the Urewera ranges) 800 miles to the north, to search for material in one of the few parts of the country where the Maori language and traditions are still preserved in daily life. Though I hadn't worked out whether it would be a documentary or a drama, I knew I wanted to learn more about these people, and to explore their view of the country I lived in.

I had grown up in the Wairarapa, a sheep farming province near the country's capital, Wellington. Each day my school bus would pass by the seat of the first Maori Parliament at Papawai, about two miles from my home. It had been established in 1897, when the surrounding community had numbered over 3 000, but less than a dozen tribal descendants lived in the vicinity now, and many of their ancestral carvings lay crumbling in the long grass.

Yet something else had given the place renown. The aspect of the carved warriors ringing the marae made it unique amongst all meeting grounds. Normal practice had them glaring out to face hostile intruders, but here the stern faces looked in towards their own people.

I wondered as I headed north if they had believed the threat would come from within. I couldn't have known the answer awaited me in Te Urewera.

Now as I travelled amongst the Tuhoe Maori, roaming from place to place, I listened to their stories of dreams and visions and ancestors, tales of kaitiaki (spiritual guardians) and patupaiarehe (the little people of the forest). It was a world of mysteries that I was drawn to, perhaps because of my Catholic upbringing. I was trying to understand that world and, in searching for this film, I suppose I was also seeking to learn more about myself.

I stayed with one old woman for six weeks and together we called on most of the kuia (old women) in the district. One had the traditional chin tattoo, but none could express that world of spirits and ancestry in a way I was able to grasp. There was one who she refused to visit. 'You wouldn't want to meet her,' she said, calling her 'the burdened one'. I was intrigued, and finally she took me to visit a little wooden house set away on one side of the marae. The woman who answered our knock was tiny, and bent almost double, as if her back still bore the loads of firewood she had carried all her life. There were no chairs and we squatted on her porch, which was cluttered with flagons of the sea water she used for blessing.

The old lady had a friendly, worn face, but to me she was closed like a book in a foreign tongue. She felt uncomfortable stumbling through the little English she knew and so we sat in embarrassed silence, while stray cats wandered in and out. I didn't know what to ask her. I wasn't an anthropologist or a journalist, coming to her with prepared questions about culture or causes. I felt so much like an alien in the Maori world, and useless because my inability to communicate made my visit seem pointless. I left after a few minutes, not wanting to intrude on her further.

Her name was Puhi. At 80 years old she kept to herself, and her world seemed a largely internal one of spirits and ancestors. After three months of searching for someone to centre the film on, I'd just about given up the idea of making it. I didn't see my subject in Puhi's uneventful daily life, but I went on visiting her, sometimes taking her gifts of spring potatoes and fishheads, which she was particularly fond of. But I never went inside her house. I felt she was too embarrassed about the mess to invite anyone in, especially a Pakeha. One day I realised there was another reason for keeping me on the veranda. I heard someone moving about inside. Out of the dark interior of the house a giant man emerged, saying nothing, his face half hidden by his hands.

This was Niki. Puhi's son was 40 years old, weighed more than 200 pounds and had been diagnosed as a paranoid schizophrenic. There were various explanations for his condition. Some said he'd been thrown from a horse and landed on his head. But all anyone really knew was that he led a quiet, normal life up to his twenties before turning inward on himself. Niki had eventually become so taciturn that some people had never heard him speak.

As if to compensate for not talking he used his hands in an expressive way, as if he were deaf and dumb. If the word coin was spoken, he'd wrap his fingers into a coin shape. He described a makutu (curse) as a silent bullet, and traced machine guns firing from his eyes. He would talk to me with one hand masking his face, the other flicking spasmodically as if trying to expel his demons. Then he would turn from me and talk to the wall, continuing our conversation.

Years before, when Niki was put into a mental hospital, Puhi spent her pension travelling 100 miles by taxi to visit him almost every weekend. This devotion defeated the authorities and they released him into her care.

Puhi had lost several children in the influenza epidemic of 1918, and she had survived both husbands — the second killed in a pub brawl. Now she had no intention of losing this middle-aged child, this man with the face of a baby buddha. She cared for him and mothered him, even if he objected, which he often did. Most of his tantrums took place on the veranda, where he'd smash the floorboards with an axe.

I accepted his violence with the same resignation as his mother and tried to help her by replacing the smashed timber with new boards. He smashed a four-by-one, so I tried a four-by-two. When he smashed this I thought I would finally defeat him by replacing the ruined boards with solid timber four inches by four inches thick. I went away to Wellington confident he could not destroy them, and when I returned I found the new boards perfectly intact — but three windows had been shattered.

On a hill overlooking Puhi's house was a dilapidated hut where I stayed, cutting back the bracken and carrying out a few basic repairs to make it liveable. It was fairly primitive, but cheap, and I was chronically short of money.

Niki had helped me move into this place. Two huge macrocarpa trees hid the back of the hut. Their two-foot-thick trunks seemed ideal to replace the unsafe corner posts, but after Heta-boy (one of the locals) helped me cut them down, we discovered we couldn't budge them. Then Niki came to the rescue. Embracing each 14-foot log like a sumo wrestler, he hauled them uphill to the holes we prepared, raised them vertical to the sun, and dropped them into position.

If spectral shadows roamed there, as the locals believed, they ignored me. The community left me alone too, except for one anonymous child who shat in the centre of the floor by way of a calling card. Looking down from the knoll I could see all the comings and goings of their lives, and my movements were clearly etched in their sights as well. I became the watcher, and the watched.

One night I was lying in the hut with the shutters open listening to the familiar sounds of the bush, the stream, and the rustle of the rats in the rafters above my head, when I heard a different noise. I knew that someone was outside. I called out 'Who's there?' My hand tightened on the machete I kept under my bed. A long silence, while I lay still, heart thudding, fear amplifying every sound so that even the blanket rustling sounded threatening. Then I saw a shadow cross the open window. I called again. Still nothing, and five minutes passed. Then a faint sound of boots shuffling on the gravel

'I dead loss.
I very sad inside me. I dead.
Feeling no good, no good. But I have to stay.'

outside the back door. Again silence, then a voice. Niki's.

I opened the door and saw him make a furtive movement. A blade flashed in the moonlight as it quickly disappeared behind him. I backed into the room and asked him to come in. Then I tried to get the Tilley lamp going, pumping furiously in the darkness, facing him all the time. I saw him making nervous movements behind his back. Trying not to sound anxious, I got up enough courage to ask him if he had an axe. 'Yeah,' he said softly. As calmly as possible I asked him if he would put it on the table. 'That's right — further away from you!' He moved it along the table, blurting out an obscure explanation, 'The buggers down there are having a party.' I think he was feeling both left out and paranoid, as they often teased him. I relaxed, built up the fire, and made Niki some tea.

Niki didn't get along with many people in the community because he got drunk easily and became aggressive, and would sometimes sneak around the houses at night peering in the windows. He was a lonely but extremely intelligent man, isolated by his erratic behaviour and his shyness. He only had three friends — his mother, their cat and the radio.

I was constantly surprised by his thoroughly bent sense of humour and love of macabre stories — a finger bone being discovered in the Nile Delta, or a shark attack

He only had three friends — his mother, their cat, and the radio.

in the Timor Sea — picked up by the aerial of an old transistor that only worked if you wobbled it. He was a hard man to fathom or be at ease with, often tense and brooding in silence for long periods. Then there were those inexplicable outbreaks of violence, even against his mother. Despite these she slept devotedly on a pile of clothing at the foot of his big double bed. I'd sometimes hear them giggling and talking well into the early morning, like children at boarding school. It was hard to imagine them separated, or decide who was the more dependent; he needed her as much as she needed to be needed.

Puhi started her day at 5 a.m. by praying for three hours, then she chopped wood and carried buckets of water, stopping every so often to murmur little prayers, raising her hand in the Ringatu homage to God. After getting the fire going she boiled the water for Niki's cup of tea. She worked hard, this bent, tiny woman, and once when she was sick I offered to help chop the wood for kindling but she refused to let me. She wouldn't let Niki help either. She was the only one who could do it properly. I had to admire her determination and stubbornness.

I was her tame Pakeha and she liked to point me out to her friends, saying, 'That's my Pakeha, the Pakeha with the blue van.' It meant I was available to drive her and Niki into town or wherever they wanted to go. Puhi didn't like to sit in the front seat. The one time I persuaded her to, she got hold of the seat-belt and somehow wrapped it several times around her neck, clutching it there tightly throughout our journey. She preferred to crouch in the back, intoning the prayers for travelling into areas where the spirits were unknown or the tribes hostile.

But Niki loved the passenger seat, gesturing in deft hand flicks as we drove, to turn left or right, accelerate, slow down or brake. It was as if without his gestures we would never have got to town safely. The machine needed the trinity: pilot, co-pilot and the spiritual support in the back.

I would take the two of them into the township of Whakatane to pick up Niki's medication from the pharmacy. Puhi liked to keep him well supplied with pills, 'downers', in case his anger became too extreme. The shop assistants in their starched white uniforms moved amid displays of glass, powder-puffs and perfumes, while the old lady in her rough-woven dress clutched her knotted walking stick. Puhi would squat near the light from the doorway in the middle of the carpet, peering into her kit (flax basket), looking for the money she could never find. Her hands were like river-stone, worn smooth by the years, and when at last she finished fossicking and found her money she would recite a little blessing over it.

Puhi means 'Special One'. Rua Kenana, known as Rua the Prophet, had given her

this name when she lived with his people, deep in the Urewera Ranges at Maungapohatu. The mountain was considered sacred by followers of the Ringatu faith (which combined Old Testament and traditional Maori beliefs), and here Rua built a circular temple with a point of entry from above, symbolising his entry from heaven. The prophet had 12 wives (seven at a time) and reputedly sired 70 children. Puhi called him uncle and worshipped the ground he walked on. Rua's community largely kept to itself until invaded by the outside world in 1917, when the government sent in armed police to arrest him. They shot one of his sons and a follower. The sound of the shooting and fear of the Pakeha sent Puhi, 17 years old, fleeing into the bush. Three days later, having lived on fernshoots and berries, she emerged carrying her newborn child.

As I gradually got to know Puhi and Niki, I realised that after all there *was* a film to be made here. Their world was not one of large events but of small details, where nothing much happened except the rituals of daily life and interdependence. To capture it I would have to film the minutiae. I decided to set up the camera and *hope* that she would walk into the frame. I felt it would underline a meditative quality that was inherent in the situation. I hoped that by filming her like this, my presence wouldn't affect the way she behaved. And just as I had to learn how to observe them, Puhi and

Niki learned to adjust to our presence in different ways.

Niki took an instant interest in our technology, questioning Steve the sound recordist about his gear. 'You must do all right with the girls with these,' he commented as he tried on the headphones, admitting sadly, 'they've never gone for me much.'

Puhi noticed the camera and immediately eyed it with suspicion, saying 'Kehua [ghosts] live in that thing.' To ease the tension we used Niki as a translator. But he loved to use his power to tease his mother, at the same time getting the upper hand on us. On the first day of shooting he told her that our lights were about to explode. Wailing she fled from the house, howling and berating us. Niki was greatly amused at the havoc he had wreaked and grinned as I pleaded and tried to reason with Puhi. It was more than a week before she allowed us back.

After a while Puhi wanted our lights on all the time. Partially blind, she would peer forward into the coal range to see if the flame was catching, then douse it with kerosene. When the fire exploded, singeing her eyebrows, she screwed up her eyes tight and muttered to herself, 'E tama, e tama! [Oh boy!]'.

I can still see her, head bent down to the table as she reached for her mug. It took her a second or two to realise her hair was being scorched by the candle, then she clucked her tongue while I moved the flame out of her way. Even then she would still manage to singe her hair somehow, and would turn to me and chuckle ruefully.

The candles she used inside the house cast strong swirling shadows that I wanted to capture. To film this we set up artificial lights run off 20 car batteries. But each time we lit the old lady, she blew her candles out. 'Don't need them now,' she said.

When it came to the shooting, Puhi's bloodymindedness nearly drove us crazy. She tolerated it all because she enjoyed our company and she liked having someone to drive her about, or to fetch and carry things. Often we would only film for a day before she would decide to visit a funeral for two or three days.

Having three extra people around tired her, but she insisted on feeding us. The more tired she grew the more hoha (grumpy) she became, and then she would think someone was casting a spell on her. Over the many difficult months that followed, I came to realise that the only way to keep her in good spirits was to film less than one week in every seven.

So I sent the film crew home and stayed on to help Puhi with her chores. Her age meant that she could no longer do many of the things she was accustomed to doing. No more horse-riding or looking for fernshoots. She was so bent that it was easier for her to store things in piles on the floor. It looked chaotic to an outsider, but she knew where she had placed every last sardine can, matchbox or pile of newspapers, each piece of firewood, jar of fat or frying pan. And she grew angry if she caught me tidying up before we filmed.

It was a year since I had started my journey. The film I had once thought would take six weeks to shoot now looked as if it would never be completed. Life was reduced to the tedium of waiting around, and the repetition of menial tasks — bucketing water by hand, scrubbing clothes in the creek. It was wearing me down and I could plan nothing. Worst of all was the constant feeling of being an outsider, a Pakeha. Because of her son's behaviour but also by choice, Puhi lived slightly apart from the rest of her community, and my film focused almost exclusively on her and Niki. I was an individual operating outside the community, and none of my previous experience equipped me to deal with the situation. Generally the community tolerated me. They were often friendly, but then I'd feel an undercurrent of criticism and suspicion and knew I had made another mistake, although I rarely discovered what it was. I had walked blind into a situation I did not understand. Now the blindfold was off and as my eyes opened to their world I became disturbingly conscious of feeling exposed.

Out of money, I returned to Wellington briefly, and it seemed as if Niki's silent bullets were following me. I woke from a dream about fire to discover that the house I was staying in was ablaze. One flatmate, our stills photographer Miles Hargest,

heroically tried to extinguish the flames with a glass of water, while the other resident escaped by jumping out a second-storey window. Although the house was largely destroyed, no one was harmed. A few days later the van caught fire on the journey back to the Ureweras. It was so badly damaged it had to be towed to the nearest garage and sold for scrap.

Back in Matahi, one of the locals joked about my constant scratching. He shaved my head and informed me I had ringworm, laughing, 'You're worse than the bloody kids.'

At the same time I caught the flu, and then conjunctivitis. As ill health wore me down and further progress on the film seemed impossible, I veered wildly between depression and anger. I knew the Maori community talked about me behind my back after our occasional misunderstandings. I knew I was considered different and felt it meant I was automatically in the wrong. I wanted to stay and finish the film, but for my sanity I had to get away. I fled to Wellington for a break, so edgy I'd cross the road when I saw a Maori. I would laugh nervously at suggestions that my run of bad luck was more than coincidence. More silent bullets followed me: every foot of film we had shot to date was ruined in processing. Strangely this disaster reinvigorated me. I saw in it a sign that I should continue. It made me realise that recording the lives of Puhi and Niki mattered more to me than my difficulties. The film was important because it documented Puhi's belief in the older values in a very fundamental way.

I began again with Steve Upston on sound and a new cameraman, Alun Bollinger. Alun felt comfortable in the area. As a boy he had often stayed at Maungapohatu and he was quick to fit in. Like me he'd only known one grandparent and he grew as fond of the old lady as I was. Nanny Puhi, as we called her, soon had the three of us at her beck and call.

One day we were set up waiting for Puhi to collect her sack of groceries from the end of the road. Hauling them over her shoulder she started wearily up the drive — and then suddenly she flung them down, broke into an angry scream, stamped her foot and squatted on the road. She had spotted us behind the meeting house and was furious we hadn't helped her. Although we didn't understand the Maori words, we knew exactly what she was saying. As Alun put it, we were naughty boys who had let their Nanny down. This incident summed up our dilemma: should we help her, or film her? Most times we managed to do both, but when she said, 'Today you have taken enough,' we knew she meant not only her energy, but her goodwill.

Soon after that incident we obtained permission to record a tangi (funeral). Feeling uncomfortable about recording between the opposing lines of callers, Steve moved off to a position where all the voices seemed to converge. It was an ideal spot to record the sound, but as he sat there in the dark it slowly registered that he was extremely close to the body.

At that moment a force hit him, so strong that it felt as if a wailing wind blew over him. He kept on saying to himself, 'I must keep control, I must keep control.' Afterwards he tried to laugh it off, but he knew that another world had crossed his own. Even now, nine years later, he is still profoundly affected by that moment. It seemed to all of us that we were at the intersection of two different worlds. And if we stood in one world, and Puhi in the other, then Niki seemed to have a foot in each, precariously straddling the divide.

By now I was becoming accustomed to his violent outbursts against his mother. One evening I returned from Wellington to find that Puhi had fled her house again. Once before she had entangled herself in an electric fence while trying to outrun Niki and had spent a large part of the night there. This time she was safe, but she only ventured back to her house when she saw my van pull up. Niki had thrown her clothes out into the rain and broken her ladder.

As we squatted outside with the camera rolling, she hid a tomahawk behind her back and as I spoke with her, she kept glancing nervously over her shoulder to check if Niki was approaching.

'He very angry, bad angry. I don't like to come in here while he's like that. He kill me then. You know one time before he came and hit me with a big stick. My neighbour go and ring the policemen but they never come.'

Puhi was so apprehensive, so scared, that even the presence of the film crew and her broken English did not inhibit her.

'You know, Vincent, I like to go away. But I know he can't light the fire. He can't cook the kai [food]. That's why I stay with him. But when I stay here he kick me, he try to break the house, he kill me then. If he's like that, then I don't like to come back. I'll go away for four days, then I come back.'

She went to the house and into the kitchen. The floor was covered in broken glass, preserved vegetables and cutlery. 'I frightened that man there. I go away to . . . aah . . . nowhere.' She knelt on the floor, picking up the debris, crying out, 'I dead loss. I very sad inside me. I dead. Feeling no good, no good. But I have to stay.'

There was nothing I could do.

Niki stood in the doorway, staring at his trousers. It seemed more than coincidence that, for all the times he chased her with axe or stick, he never caught her.

Puhi made tea and asked Niki something in Maori. He replied angrily in English,

'I don't care. It don't worry me, I'll stay like a rat, that's all I care.'

When the crew finally finished and left, Puhi became more dependent on me. She got bronchitis. I rented a house up the road with electricity and running water, and she and Niki came to live with me. It felt strange. I was only 23 and had never had to look after anyone. I spent my time drawing water for Niki's bath, taking them into town and generally taking care of them. At night we'd be in our beds, Niki's rugged snoring on one side of the room, Puhi's fine whistling in her sleep on the other. One morning Niki mentioned quietly, 'I heard the bird last night. Someone is going to die.' That day a tohunga, an old carver who had once crafted the guardians of his marae, passed away.

Three days later his tangi was held. The sky was overcast and it had rained off and on throughout the day. We waited for his funeral entourage to arrive. One, then two hours went by before it finally appeared and at that very moment the sky broke open and rain poured down on us. When the hearse drew up and its doors opened, the rain stopped instantly.

Two rainbows appeared in the sky, one unusually intense, arched over the other. They carried the coffin to the whare mate (house of the dead) and the rainbows

disappeared. I was spellbound, but the locals were much more matter of fact about it all. They knew that such things happened when someone of the dead man's stature had passed away.

In the cold spring of that week, several of the old people died. One of them was Puhi's closest friend. I found Puhi sitting on the floor in the corridor. In despair, she was hacking off her hair with a blunt knife.

The rain beat down on our faces as Puhi called to the mourners stoically waiting at the tangi, their scarf-covered heads wreathed in leaves, their black dresses trailing in the mud. The death of this neighbour proved a turning point for Puhi. It seemed to take away her will to live. Puhi had always determinedly looked after herself and others, but now for the first time she moved away from her home permanently, to be looked after by kinfolk in Auckland. More than two years after I had begun, I also left the valley. It was time to edit the material.

I could never have known that I would see Puhi only one more time. I took my film to her step-daughter's home in Auckland, to show her and Niki. The three-pin plug on the old projector I was using fused. Puhi was not surprised. She just muttered, 'Hmm . . . meant to be.' She never saw the film, although I took it back to the valley and showed it to a group of elders. Shortly afterwards, when I was overseas, Puhi died.

I did not hear of her death until I returned. Of all the people I had known, Pakeha and Maori, she was the one I most wanted to say goodbye to, and I wished I had been at her tangi.

I remembered how she would greet me when I went away to Wellington, how she would welcome me home: 'Mokopuna ma, mokopuna ma [my (white) grandchild]. We very moke moke [lonely] since you've been away.' My father's mother died when I was very young, so Puhi was the only grandmother I had known. She'd taken me into her family with the philosophical acceptance that age sometimes brings. I was close to my own mother, but I sometimes resented her judgments and always I felt the need to earn her respect. Puhi didn't judge, and with her I could simply be.

A few years later I went back to the valley to look for her grave. The area was covered in long grass and I could find no sign of it. It was as if she had been absorbed back into the earth. Puhi, the caller on the marae, had herself been called. I thought of the proverb in the Maori Planter's Calendar:

In autumn many gather, in spring one plants alone.

I had been young, uncertain and confused when I first came to Te Urewera, and in almost three years I had learnt much more than I thought possible. Puhi had given me a gift that was fundamental yet intangible, a precious kit that had been woven in pain, in love and care. Wherever I have been since I have carried it with me.

Like the weathered ancestral figures I had seen as a child, Puhi looked inwards to family and home. I realised those cracked wooden sentinels on the marae near my home faced in towards their own, not in anger or fear of threat but in love. They were the peacemakers.

Returning to Te Urewera, I found that all along the valley the same houses stood. Different people lived in them now, but their faces were familiar. I had wandered into another land, and this was no longer the Matahi I knew. It was as if the people I'd known here had vanished through a mirror, and yet somehow they remained, staring out from the faces that greeted me. Everyone was related. As one person passed on or moved away, there would always be another in their stead, living in the same house, walking the same land.

I recalled part of a conversation I had heard in Matahi: 'When I feel harassed I always think of myself as "he", not "I". And then I look to see what "he" is doing. It reminds me of how others see me and of my own lack of importance. It reminds me I'm just part of a community, a small part of the whole.'

In 1989 I traced Niki Takao to an Auckland hostel for the intellectually handicapped — the only institution that would take him in. He had his own shed out the back and had held a job in the city since Puhi died. Sometimes in the summer he ran away and camped in the bush beside the city railway tracks. 'I rather prefer the country,' he said. 'The city's too quick, too quick, it's not the same.' But at the end of summer he would return, have a hot bath and stay on at the hostel through the winter months.

More than seven years after her death I finally made my peace with Puhi. It was auspiciously misty the day three Tuhoe elders came to hear me read this story, in an attic room overlooking a normally sunny bay in Auckland. As I began, a tapping started at the window, like the gentle knock of a walking stick against the pane. Talking about Puhi, I found I was missing her so much I began to blubber. As I grabbed for a handkerchief and found only a sheet of computer paper to mop my face with, I realised that the others were crying too. Like me they had not been at her tangi, and their farewells had been left unspoken. As I finished the story the tapping stopped and one of the elders broke into a chant.

In a ceremony normally performed in the house of the deceased on the morning of a tangi, he said a karakia (prayer). The house was finally swept, the air cleared, and the old spirits laid to rest:

> *Rest Puhi,*
> *rest with those who passed on.*
> *Rest with those who left you*
> *the gifts which they passed on,*
> *to leave behind when you join them.*
> *Rest with the many*
> *of the Tuhoe in the night.*

———

There is a Maori saying which roughly translated means 'my past lies before me'. Listening to Puhi's casual conversations with her ancestors had led me to wonder about my own people. About my parents and their stories of the past, about the places and people they came from, and the land they worked at inhabiting; about the juncture of events that form us.

I drew on the claustrophobia and isolation I had felt while making In Spring One Plants Alone *to write a new film, set in a rural Catholic community, making use of aspects of my childhood, making use of the familiar.*

Part II

VIGIL

'The Dispossessed' —
Jewish refugees in
Palestine, 1946.
(Cornelius Ryan)

A PRELUDE

We are born from the past. Sometimes when I consider the way my parents met I am surprised at how big a part fate and circumstances played in my own birth. My mother was born Edith Rosenbacher in Hamburg in 1923. She was brought up in an era and in a way that seem foreign to us, a world where children lived apart from the adults. It was only natural that my mother and her sister Ines grew close to their maids. My mother was especially fond of Ilma, a plump, uneducated countrywoman who called Edith 'Muschi' (pussy), and entertained her charges with stories about her many romances (real or imaginary, it was hard to know).

Edith's father had inherited wealth but he was a poor businessman, and although they were not a wealthy family they were comfortable in a world of certain values, *Gemütlichkeit* and a close circle of friends and relatives. One of their cousins was Doctor Albert Schweitzer, and the story was told in the family of how he saved Edith's mother's life when he jumped into a river to rescue her after she had fallen off her bicycle.

Like many others the Rosenbachers considered themselves more German than

Berlin, 1932. Boarding school.

Hamburg, 1931. Edith and Ines.

Leo and Gertrud Rosenbacher, my mother Edith and Ines.

Jewish — indeed, Edith's father had won the Iron Cross in the Great War. But it was becoming harder to close one's eyes to what was happening in Germany, as Jews began disappearing without trace. My mother stood on the balcony of her house above Eppendorferland Strasse. 'I could see the Brown Shirts, the S.A., marching past with their arms swinging, their boots on, and they were singing a marching song. They were a terrifying sight. It seemed to me as if there was mob rule.'

For their own safety Gentile friends began avoiding the Rosenbachers in the street, and Ilma had to leave them and go to work for an Aryan family. The Nazi pressure on the Jewish people in Hamburg grew more intense until the Rosenbachers were forced to sell their home and furniture, for a fraction of their real value.

All Jewish children had been expelled from the state school system, so Edith was sent with her sister Ines to a Berlin boarding school. While their mother took a room near the school, their father emigrated to Palestine and prepared for his family to join him. Edith always remembered the kindness of her teachers; it seemed as if they were deliberately trying to hide the horror of what was going on beyond the boarding school walls. After two years in Berlin their mother managed to obtain passports to get out of Germany. It wasn't until many years later that Edith heard a story about the fate of her fellow students and the teachers who remained behind. According to her informant, the Nazis had forced them to lie down on the road outside the school, and had then driven over them.

The departure from Germany was the beginning of a series of exiles for my mother. After crossing by train to the Italian port of Trieste, my grandmother was able to arrange their passage to Palestine to join her husband. But at the last moment she became too ill to make the voyage. It was another difficult parting, waving goodbye from the quayside at Trieste as her two young daughters sailed away to start their new life without her. When asked to describe the look on my grandmother's face as they departed, my mother was reluctant to answer and began to cry, the memory still raw after almost 60 years.

On board the ship the sisters became everybody's favourites. They spent their time running and playing around the deck and stuffing themselves with food and sweets given to them by fellow passengers. The sadness at leaving their mother gave way to a sense of excitement about joining their father and experiencing at first hand the camels, donkeys, palm trees and deserts seen in books and films.

Their father met them in Palestine and took them to a small Jewish settlement in Galilee near Haifa, where above them in the hills the girls saw the black goatskin tents of the Bedouins. Grandfather Rosenbacher was trying to earn money doing farm work,

but he was really too old and too impractical to make a success of it. He had no home and it was impossible for him to look after his daughters alone. Ines went to live on a kibbutz and Edith was taken in by a friend of his, Doctor Felsenbach, and started to absorb her strange new surroundings.

'There was a little clump of trees in front of the house, and there were Arabs who came to consult the doctor. They used to camp overnight. I would press my nose against the window and stare at their donkeys and their babies. They used to put the babies on the ground and all the flies would crawl around their eyes and mouth and they never thought to wave them away. I remembered how exasperated Dr Felsenbach would get, because the Arabs would sometimes drink a whole bottle of medicine at once, not following directions. They rarely paid, but were generous with gifts of bantam hens, eggs and vegetables. He learned Arabic to speak to them, and he loved them just as much as he loved his Jewish patients.'

Realising she was extremely shy and might find it difficult to learn Hebrew, Dr Felsenbach organised five Jewish girls of Edith's age to visit. When they arrived they pushed her out of the house and took her up the street, pointing out things to her in Hebrew. 'Of course they could speak no other language and they'd say to me, this is a tree . . . this is a road . . . and this is a house.'

From my father's photo album — Egyptian water-carrier (left)
and a citadel at Abassia (right).

Within three or four months Edith was speaking the language, and it was during this period that she took the name Jehudit (Hebrew for Judith). After two years of waiting and wondering, her mother finally arrived in Palestine and the family was reunited.

The Jewish people had thought that the British, who held mandate over Palestine through the League of Nations, were going to establish an independent Jewish state. But the White Paper eventually issued stated that the whole country would in fact become an independent Arab state, and stipulated that the Jewish minority was not to exceed 30 percent of the population. Jewish leaders were disappointed, but when war broke out they encouraged the young to join the British army, hoping their support for the war effort would earn them a greater say in Palestine's fate after the war. Although their enlistments were initially refused by the British fighting forces, they were later allowed to join transport and supply units.

One of those who joined up was Edith Rosenbacher. She was posted to the Mena Desert camp near Cairo, where the bombed and broken down trucks were repaired, refitted and returned to the front. Her job was to bring in the trucks from outlying areas to the workshops. Frequently they had to be towed and so she often spent days behind the wheel of trucks with no brakes and shattered windscreens, wrapped up in scarves

Egypt, 1943. Mena army barracks.

trying to keep out the sand that choked her and stung her eyes.

From the beginning, Edith liked army life. She liked drilling because she enjoyed the unity of movement, and with all the young women in her unit much the same age, she began to love the sense of camaraderie in the Mena barracks. Their shared laughter would break the monotony of the slow drift back to the workshops, when the convoy passed through Arab villages and the boys lifted their robes to expose their genitals in a half-serious gesture of contempt.

Across the other side of the world my father Pat joined up fully expecting to die. He was 33 years of age, already old for a soldier, and he had memories of seeing the broken men returning from the Great War. Most of his life had been spent in rural New Zealand. Tall, debonair, with big hands and feet that measured exactly a foot long, he knew how to charm and he was good with words. His army mates paid him to write their letters home, hoping to win back their girlfriends from the Yankee soldiers stationed in New Zealand.

One day in 1942 Pat was part of a thirteen-mile-long convoy passing through northern Syria to deliver supplies to the Russians, when his truck caught fire. It was

Egypt, 1942.

carrying 600 gallons of petrol.

He tried to put out the flames but the fire extinguisher was faulty, and the petrol ignited and began to blaze fiercely. Realising that the soft sand on either side of the narrow bitumen road would prevent the convoy from passing the burning truck and hold it up for hours, Pat managed to drive clear of the road. Over a third of his body was badly burned.

On the back of a lorry, he was driven across the desert to the village of Deir el Zoir, where he was cared for in an Arab-run hospital so poorly staffed that he cried out for water for over two hours and nobody came. His face stuck to the pillowcase, which was covered with the blood of a previous patient. Next day his bandaged body was still in its burnt uniform — until his unit captain gave him his own pyjamas.

When he was discharged from hospital after three months the Army issued him with a .38 revolver, as his hands were so severely burned he could no longer use a rifle.

The sculptor Henry Moore received a bullet wound during the war, and he subsequently became obsessed with making holes in the free-form bodies that he carved. Like Moore, my father would remain obsessed with his wounds, and the fire that caused them.

By January 1945 the Second World War in the Middle East was over and my father was waiting to be sent back home to New Zealand. Because there was nothing to do, he and a gunner friend decided to take a trip to Cedars, north of Beirut. The gunner had arranged for him to go out with the mayor's daughter.

Their train arrived at the junction where the lines branched off to Beirut and Jerusalem, and they went to the army canteen, the only place still open at two o'clock in the morning. The food was terrible and the only spare seats were next to a pretty, softspoken ATS girl who generously offered to share her sandwiches. This was Edith Rosenbacher, on her way home from Mena camp in Egypt to be discharged. The gunner had a train to catch and arranged to meet up with my father in Beirut a few days later, but as he left he took another long look at the ATS girl. 'Watch it,' he warned Pat.

Later Edith wrote, 'I had this little thought in my mind that the tall Kiwi might come in handy to carry my bags.' But whatever thoughts she had, after the New Zealander helped with her luggage, he decided to join her on the train to Jerusalem. He stayed there a week, going out with her every day — and standing up the laconic gunner who left him a succinct note: 'You bastard.'

A week later in the streets of Jerusalem, Edith turned to Pat and asked mischievously, 'How would you like to take me back to New Zealand?' He didn't answer her, and he never did ask her to marry him, but instead set about making practical arrangements for their wedding.

Before my father returned to Cairo my mother went home to Haifa, and they agreed to meet under the clock outside Barclay's Bank there to say goodbye. He waited for an hour, not knowing she'd been very ill. Pat realised then that he did not know my mother's last name or where she lived. He had no idea of how to get in touch with her again. He was just about to go when he saw her running through the crowds towards him (and here I am decades later urging her to run faster, urging him not to go yet, otherwise they will never see each other again and their story will never be finished).

My father returned to his unit. He started making arrangements for Edith to join him, so they could be married at the Catholic chapel at Maadi, one of three New Zealand legal army marriage areas in Cairo at the time. Once they were married, Edith would automatically become a New Zealand citizen and be provided with free passage to New Zealand.

But the Egyptian authorities were reluctant to give permission now that she was a civilian and would not allow the Jewish girl back into Egypt. A brigadier and a colonel tried to help him by sending many letters requesting that she be allowed in, but nothing happened.

Throughout his letters to his fiancée, one can see his growing despair, his moods swinging between optimism and the fear that they would never meet again, never marry. It seemed as if nobody was on their side. The Rosenbachers found it strange that a man of 38 would not be married and have children back in New Zealand and they thought that like many soldiers, he was lying about his past. If their suspicions were not enough, his soldier mates were advising him against the marriage too.

Despite all the opposition, my father believed everyone who stood against them was wrong, and he wrote to her, 'The story of you and I is a specific story. It merits specific attention. Outsiders must, of necessity, view it in a general way.'

Somehow my father had to try and break the monotony of official refusal. He went to the department of the Egyptian chargé d'affaires day after day, slowly ingratiating himself with the clerical staff. He explained he'd worked in a similar department in New Zealand and, lying outrageously, told them how efficiently he thought they kept their records. He asked if he could look at their filing system in order to copy their methods for use back home and flattered, they agreed. He suggested they start at the W's. In that section he found what he was looking for: all the letters he and his superiors had sent, each one rejected, each page slashed in blue pencil.

He studied the rest of his file until he had a complete picture of his case, then on the fourth morning he arrived early and went into the office of the Egyptian chargé d'affaires. He sat down and put his feet up on the table, placed his revolver on the desk in front of him and waited. Eventually the chargé d'affaires arrived. My father asked him to be seated, motioned to the gun and assured him that four years at the front had made him an excellent shot.

He repeated his request to have Edith come to Egypt for a fortnight. This time the chargé d'affaires agreed, but my father was not about to leave the office until he was certain his bride would be arriving, so he watched while the official sent the cables. It was a tense time for both men, but after permission had been given, both relaxed, and the Egyptian poured a drink and proposed a toast to the 'cheekiest Kiwi I have ever met'. After downing his drink, Pat picked up his unloaded revolver and rushed to the nearest bar to celebrate. Even now, after hearing this story for years, I am still amused by the Errol Flynn bravado of it all and moved by his acting so desperately out of a real love for a woman he had only seen for a week.

My mother arrived in Cairo the next day, and after their marriage they left for New Zealand on a crowded troop ship. There were 5000 men, and six married couples. But at first only married officers were allowed cabins. The lower ranks had to eat and sleep below decks while their wives slept in cabins and ate at the officers' table. It was a ridiculous situation for a honeymooning couple, only made tolerable by a

coincidence. The priest who had married them was also on the ship and, realising the problem, told them his cabin was at their disposal. (Eventually, after considerable pressure had been brought to bear on the ship's authorities, the six couples were granted cabins.)

For the second time in her life, my mother was heading off into an uncertain future, into exile at the bottom of the world, not knowing what to expect. 'I'd been told that in New Zealand everybody rode horses and you had to learn to ride, and in no time I'd learn to speak Maori, just as I had learned to speak Hebrew when I went to Palestine.' But my father had no illusions. He had been away fighting for five years and constantly warned her of how little money he had. 'Ever since the Phoenicians invented money, life has become more complicated,' he wrote just before she joined him in Egypt. 'Our future from the financial angle is the only thing that makes me despondent. Whether we shall be successful will depend so much upon ourselves.'

In New Zealand Edith, who had become Jehudit in Israel, now became Judy. She and my father settled on a piece of land in Morison's Bush, the same area in which his grandfather Thomas, a surveyor's labourer, had settled 100 years before. Thomas had chosen the land because it reminded him of the soft, green countryside of Ireland. One day the whole valley was destroyed in a bushfire and the trees never returned, the land was never as soft and lush again. But from the fire he gained a wife. She was three months pregnant, the widow of a young man who died fighting the blaze. Eventually she and my grandfather had five children of their own. But then, within the space of a month, the choking sickness (a diphtheria epidemic) killed four of their children. Coming home from burying their last child, they found their house had burned to the ground. Tenaciously, Thomas Ward rebuilt his house and he and his wife had more children.

My father had that same determination. Before the war he'd been a labourer, a footballer, a bouncer, an insurance salesman, an office worker and he'd been to university, but now the state of his health limited his options. On medical advice he had to work outdoors, and so he came to realise his last dream — to turn a derelict piece of land into a perfect show farm.

It was a hard life. Home was a one-room shack-on-wheels, with small boxes for chairs, a large one for a table. They had no electricity, no water and a patch of gorse for a lavatory. Judy thought how far it was from the servants, the silverware, the classical piano lessons of Hamburg — to her, the farm seemed primeval, at the edge of the

Home, 1946. The shed on wheels.

earth. The weather was freezing and she felt the cold keenly in the lightweight clothes she'd brought from Palestine.

She found it hard adjusting to a country where drinking was a major part of the social fabric. Limited licensing hours had given rise to the phenomenon of the 'six o'clock swill' — the rapid drinking during the brief period between knock off time and the time the pubs closed.

'I'd never seen such drinking — it was not part of the Jewish lifestyle. It seemed every time people went to town, they went to a hotel.'

Even the conversation was like nothing she had ever heard before: 'I'd never seen racing in my life, never knew anything about it. It was totally foreign, almost alien to me, and racing was talked about all the time. People loved to place bets on horses. Every Saturday, all day long, Pat's family had the races going on the radio. If they didn't go to the track, they were placing bets on the telephone.'

And then there was the farming talk, and the news about neighbours, people she didn't know. 'I found it difficult to join in the conversations. I just sat there like a shadow, a silent shadow.'

It was a lonely time. She was five miles from town, had no car, knew almost no one. The local people were friendly, but like many New Zealanders, reserved. There

Hamburg, 1906. My great-grandmother (second from left) *and great-grandfather* (far right) *in their drawing room.*

Grandmother, grandfather and Dad at the Winter Race
Meeting. Wellington, 1951.

was no heating. It seemed to rain all winter in this cold bleak land, and being poor and pregnant made it seem all the bleaker. She and Pat had little money: on one occasion all they had to live on for a fortnight was two shillings. After about a year they moved into an old schoolhouse, where they had their first child. Judy had two children before she had an armchair, three children before she had hot water.

Seventeen years younger than Pat, she sometimes felt the age gap made him regard her more like one of his children than his wife. My father spent most of his time working — working for others to get money, or working on his own land.

He was a man totally driven by his vision of creating the perfect farm. Typically, despite being warned that it was impossible to turn this derelict piece of land into a show farm, he worked doggedly to prove everyone wrong. The land was covered in gorse, manuka and native grass, and he spent all day burning and cutting, clearing back new pasture, and killing rabbits. These plagued the farm in such numbers that the first time poison was laid for them he found 280 carcasses the next morning.

At night he rebuilt the old house. One evening while burning paint off with a blowtorch, he was interrupted by a neighbour. Within seconds a flame crept under the eaves and ignited the house.

My mother tried to get hold of the fire brigade. The phone was on a party line and when she tried to call she found a couple already on the line. 'I was too panic stricken to be thinking clearly, or to be rational enough to actually say "Listen here, we've got a house fire, let me have the line." So I kept on saying "Working? Working?" — just to let them know someone else was wanting to speak. I didn't have the cheek to tell them to get off. I was a very, very shy young woman.'

Within an hour the house had burned to the ground. They had just enough time to rescue the sleeping baby and two toddlers, some bedding, singed photographs and a pile of accounts which, ironically, turned out to be their bills.

The local people organised a concert to raise money for my parents and brought them more household belongings than they could ever use. Only one wall of the house remained, and from that my father began again. The place that he built became my childhood home.

MAKING VIGIL

I was not a lonely child, but an alone child. I was the youngest, and because my sisters and brother were mostly away at boarding school, I spent a lot of time on my own. The world I lived in was partly based in reality, partly the creation of my imagination.

My father was 50 when I was born, and by then he had shaped his farm. But the cliffs at the far end of the property remained untamed, their edges crumbling. As a young boy I watched from a distance while my father stood at the precipice, tossing rubbish and the bodies of dead sheep down into the forest. Later, when I was 10 or so, my brother and sister took me to the cliffs and, as a practical joke, abandoned me on a plateau half way down. It is a snapshot in my memory now — I'm screaming for them to come and get me, eyeing the dark bush below, too scared to make my way up.

Once I saw a hawk dive out of the sky and pluck the eyes from a live lamb. I was not surprised because like most children growing up in the country, I accepted the farm's casual violence as part of the natural order. I tried to impress my brother with the number of birds I had killed, and happily helped my father in the bloody business

of docking and tailing lambs. Again, I see myself in vivid unconnected fragments, fragments where I am walking in the shadow of my father's war stories, dressed in his army jacket, wearing my great uncle's World War One medals, carrying a baseball bat and a .22 rifle with 200 rounds of ammunition, full of seriousness and purpose as I go to check my opossum lines, or wage imaginary battles against sheep who remained blissfully unaware of their ignominious defeat.

I played in the shadows of other people's imaginations: Scott and his Ivanhoe, Grimms' fairy stories and the Knights of the Round Table. The derelict woolshed metamorphosed into a necromancer's sinister lair where a screaming opossum might become a banshee, poked into fury by my younger self.

A stubborn, clumsy boy, I loved contact sports and brawling, although why I liked fighting puzzles me. I wasn't very good at it and was forever being knocked out. By the time I was 14 I'd been concussed nine times, which might explain the brevity of my career as a Catholic altar boy — I was so vague and preoccupied that I would ring the gong at the wrong time during Mass.

Although I wasn't particularly religious I was drawn to the apocalyptic engravings in my grandfather's leatherbound Bible. I imagined I saw demons rising up out of the flaming fields to peals of thunder as my father burned back the barley stubble. Fire

attracted me, and I felt a compulsion to watch as he set alight the pyres of stillborn lambs. Once a skyrocket went off in my hands, and it took me a while to notice it had burned into my flesh like a brand. The burn was minor, but the incident foreshadowed the fires that were to pursue me, just as they had stalked my father and great-grandfather.

My childhood was not extraordinarily eventful. It's the emotional intensity with which I viewed the world that dominates my memories. I clearly recall storming off after an argument to lie in a field with arms outstretched imagining that I was being filmed by the eye of God.

In *Vigil*, I wanted to recreate my childhood perception of the world I had inhabited. I wanted to see a small, intense child on a farm by himself, combating fierce nightmares and fantasising victories over imaginary foes. At the same time I wanted to convey how a child seems to see the real world in oblique glimpses, and like a detective gathering clues, has to work out what is going on about him.

For a long time I just kept notebooks, writing down ideas, or characters, or images, trying to find a story. Gradually the child began to form and it turned into a girl. How do I explain this, even to myself, now? When I was young I didn't mix much with girls, and yet I could remember for a long time fantasising about having a female

companion, one I could play with or go hunting with. Perhaps those relationships you miss out on in childhood are those you search for as an adult, and I was giving form and flesh to my imaginary friend.

I began creating the character of the young girl Toss from parts of my sister and girlfriend and from the bones of childhood. For her mother Elizabeth, co-writer Graeme Tetley and I developed a woman whose estrangement from the land echoed my mother's sense of isolation and frustration at this strange new country. Gradually it became obvious that having a girl as the central character was a bonus because there would be a greater tension in having a triangle of male intruder, the young widow, and her daughter as rival.

Childhood is a common theme in New Zealand writing. Perhaps this is due to the relative newness of the national identity, and 'rites of passage' stories reflect this coming of age. Maybe we are attracted to the theme because New Zealand is so remote that when we venture into the world outside we do so as innocents.

With *Vigil* began a partnership with John Maynard, who had been an arts administrator before becoming a producer. Before that he had done a stint in London as a builder, and it was no doubt this background that made him liken my scriptwriting method to constructing a twelve-storey building on its side, only to hoist it vertical by rope, detailing all the parts of it before looking at the whole structure. While John deals in broad strokes, I'm obsessive about detail.

Hunting for a location confirmed our differences. I had an image in my mind, but it was made up of various images I had seen or imagined, and that was the problem I had set myself; we were searching for an ideal location that was composed of many different places. Something that didn't really exist except as a composite assembled from memories.

I travelled 18 000 miles to try and find this product of my imagination and it seemed that I had driven along every road and track in both islands. John joined this quest but after six days cooped up in a car with an increasingly possessed film-maker he fled. I had been searching for so long that I couldn't give up. Not long afterwards, at John's suggestion, I investigated a horseshoe-shaped valley in Taranaki, and realised I had found my location. The hills were burnt, eroded by time, primitive looking and yet not so large that they would dwarf the actors below. The valley had everything I needed to tell my story, even down to the knoll where there would be a hut overlooking the farmhouse.

Around this time I was invited to serve on a film festival jury in Paris and I made a detour to Chartres cathedral, another journey influenced by my childhood. I remembered sitting in front of our gramophone listening to a recording of Charles Laughton describing in long, succulent sentences the extraordinary beauty of those stained glass windows. The light and colours were as exquisite as I anticipated, but more profound was the impact of the cathedral's acoustics, which were strongly reminiscent of those in my valley. Characteristically noises were soft and muted, but certain sounds became amplified, and those close by were extraordinarily clear, like drops of water falling into a still pool.

This was how I wanted Toss to hear the world: muffled, unclear, then suddenly rent by the scream of a hawk or the thud of a knife into wood, sharp and lucid, reverberating down the valley like the echoes at Chartres.

I remembered the leading hand of the construction crew building the set, knee-deep in mud, screaming at the damp, claustrophobic walls of the valley, answered only by an endlessly mocking echo. There were no standing buildings in the valley, and so we had to bring in everything we needed and build from scratch the woolshed, farmhouse and hut on the hill. It was a lonely and eerie location, the ground littered with dead sheep and the sky filled with hawks. The valley walls were crumbling because the farmer who owned the land had used farming loans to cut down and burn the trees that held the cliffs up. It was the perfect environment in which to convey how the harsh pragmatism of the farmer, killing and maiming everything that moves, except his beloved sheep, sets him forever against nature — and how nature has its revenge.

The set had a medieval feel, as if we were seeing it through Toss's eyes after she had been influenced by *Grimms' Fairy Tales*. When it was not looking how I imagined it should, I waited until the crew was away and went into one of the sets and destroyed the interior with an adze and crowbar. This pointed act of finality might have sent some art directors into a fury, but Kai Hawkins shrugged tolerantly.

Over two years, I must have visited several hundred schools looking for the child who would play Toss, looking for the face I had in my mind. Eventually, after workshopping 50 children we narrowed it down to five possibilities, one a timid part-Maori girl. Not only was she good for the part but it seemed that the whole workshop experience was a breakthrough for her, allowing her to express a part of herself she'd never had the chance to explore. Then she stopped coming, and a few weeks later, crying, she rang to explain. Her father had decided that we were making a blue movie.

I finally found my Toss in Fiona Kay. She was a bookworm, a scrawny city kid who hated walking barefoot on the grass and read insatiably between every take — unlike the tomboy I had in mind. The women in the film crew were amused because it seemed to them that Fiona bore more than a passing resemblance to me. And I wondered if I

had really scanned the faces of 40 000 schoolgirls unconsciously searching for my clone.

I knew it was going to be a difficult shoot. Like my father warning his fiancée about the hazards of their life in New Zealand, I cautioned the crew before they came on location. I said that it would be the most miserable place on earth, that for three months they would be soaking wet most of the time and they could expect no entertainment because we would be so far from any town. I told them they would end up hating it. Reverse psychology, I thought.

We were cold, miserable and up to our knees in mud, and it was impossible to keep the wardrobe clean and dry. Even when the sky cleared, rain machines were used. And all that time there were long periods spent doing nothing while cameraman Alun Bollinger and I waited for the right light, for special reflections from the dam, or for the storm-swept look of the engravings I had seen in our family Bible.

Much of my attention was concentrated on Fiona, who appeared in almost every scene. She was very bright and astute, with an inner strength that helped her last the distance in sometimes difficult conditions. The work was also emotionally tough, and towards the end of the shoot Fiona became so tired she was often close to tears. I could understand her ringing her mother some evenings, wanting to go home.

I've heard it said that children who are brought up in a one-parent household are more determined, but it was only after I had cast Fiona that I discovered she had not seen her father since she was two.

Most of the time on the set she was with adults, always the small child at the dinner table, the figure in the back of the car pretending to be invisible, but listening all the time, relentlessly curious about people's relationships, writing down juicy details in her notebook like a secret gossip columnist. Keeping it for further reference or blackmail, I wondered? Certainly at times she was no angel. If I made her do something she didn't like she'd often kick me in the shins.

Later, when the film came out in Australia, her father rang the distributors, asking for tickets to see his daughter for the first time in 10 years. During that time he had always been a postal address ahead of her attempts to track him down. What did he think as he watched her on the screen?

Often I had seen my father, like the character in the film, sling an army bag over his shoulder and head off to some far corner of his farm. When he visited the set I got him to play an extra in the funeral scene. He's always had a special fondness for funerals, constantly talking about them, delivering eulogies at them, and in later years turning first to the obituary column in the newspaper. He enjoyed imagining his own funeral, pondering who would turn up to see him off, and perhaps he recognised the funeral scene in *Vigil* as one he had imagined.

Now 83, my father still likes misquoting Yeats: 'The old men stared at their reflections in the water and said all that is beautiful is dead.' 'If you think about it,' he says, 'they've outlived everyone they knew, everything that they once held dear.'

By the time he appeared in *Vigil*, he'd sold the farm. But my father was still the perfectionist who used to worry about the symmetry of his fences in his dreams. He took one look at the fence lines on the set, and bemoaned the poor workmanship.

Vigil was completed and I took it to Cannes, afterwards travelling for a while in Germany. I didn't see the valley again for three years and when I did, it was like revisiting Te Urewera after I'd finished *In Spring One Plants Alone*. It seemed as if I was stepping out of time and into some fiction which eerily paralleled reality.

During the *Vigil* shoot the set had been infused with life; now the hunter's hut and the farmhouse were crumbling away. Yet the place evoked a sense of people having lived and died here, people I knew — I might have been viewing the ruins on my grandparents' property. It was as if the characters in *Vigil* had found an existence beyond the film, had broken free to live out their lives in this place and left behind a personal history. Another childhood had been created in this valley, a world of shadows that had become as real as my actual childhood.

———

Germany had always attracted me. I thought of my mother as a child boarding the ship at Trieste, leaving her mother behind. Steadfastly she refused ever to go back to the country from which she'd fled. I wondered also about her childhood home in Hamburg and tried unsuccessfully to find it and to trace something of her past.

There I was introduced to one of her contemporaries and found a quirky idea that pursued me until it became the starting point of a new film.

Part III

THE NAVIGATOR

The old man had been a member of the Hitler Youth in Hamburg when my mother had fled the city, and they were the same age. He had also joined the Luftwaffe at the same time my mother had enlisted with the British Army. Now, ironically, I was going out with his liberal daughter. I glanced at the model Messerschmitt 109 resting on the mantelpiece in his Hamburg home and surprised him by casually identifying it. I had gained his confidence and he soon opened up to me, while my friend argued with him about a recent issue of a neo-Nazi magazine she found lying on his sofa.

Far from being unsettled by the fact he was a Nazi, I found that I liked him, as he reminded me of my father. For both of them the war had been so important. The old German had been an ace in the Luftwaffe, flying 15 different types of plane, many of them captured from the enemy. These he had test-piloted, the better to defeat them. Near the war's end he had been captured and interned in Russia. He talked only of the war, and I realised that just as it had changed my mother and father, so irrevocably it had changed his life and still haunted him.

The trip to Germany had been important to me. I passed through medieval villages and while I was hitch-hiking, tried to cross a seven-lane autobahn. Although I had managed to get safely across three lanes of rush hour traffic, the remaining four were impossible to traverse. I was marooned. And as I waited on the median strip it struck me how it would feel if you were dropped from the Middle Ages into the twentieth century and were stranded there like I was. The notion stayed in my mind, and began to expand into the story of *The Navigator*.

Exploring the idea from the perspective of my ancestors, I delved into a past that was part invention and part research, to find out what kind of people they had been. I was trying to pull together the pieces.

My father often spoke of his Celtic origins and told of the village his Irish forebears had come from — although with each of the many tellings, he'd forget the location and the village would shift from county to county. At 80, he finally went to Ireland to find where his ancestors did actually spring from. When he traced the site he found the village had disappeared and the land was now covered with forest. As he searched through parish records I imagined him uncovering medieval manuscripts, and therefore it was his voice I heard retelling the story of *The Navigator*.

I worked on the screenplay for two years before going to Britain for casting and further research. While I was there I met my mother's half-sister, yet another of her family who had been exiled by the war. Far from the strong, able-bodied image I had from my mother, who had not seen her in decades, Aunt Margot was rather frail, dressed in many layers of clothing, living in a decaying house in Golders Green.

In her face I saw an older version of my mother's. As she turned to usher me through the corridor cluttered with books and newspapers I noticed that her leg was swollen and every step seemed painful to her. She steered me into a mahogany-coloured living-room, which was full of hundreds of yellowing letters scattered over the floor in haphazard bundles, her connection with family spread all over the globe. I told her about my film. She listened, full of concentration, smoking one cigarette after another, stubbing each one out half-finished. Her training in psychoanalysis came to the fore as question by question she pinned me down on what my film was actually about.

'A brotherhood of men from the fourteenth century save their village from the Black Death.'

'No. I don't believe that is it,' she replied, patiently waiting out my silence as I tried to think of another answer, leaning intently towards me, one cheek resting in her hand just like my mother when she watches television. Her eyes never left my face as I struggled to come up with something more precise. Finally I offered a definition of the film as the twentieth century seen through a medieval lens.

Dissatisfied, she shook her head and stubbed out another cigarette. I began to realise that we were solving a riddle together, 90 minutes of story to be crystallised into

Aunt Margot and Grandmother. 1919.

a phrase so clear that it would drive the film. Then in a burst of clarity I realised what it was that had kept me going for two years. Written by a sceptic, my story was about faith — about the basic need to maintain belief in something, anything, no matter what.

I was surprised that my answer seemed important to her. Then I remembered that Aunt Margot had studied psychoanalysis in Germany before the war, and for years had tried to get into medical schools all over Britain so that she could practise as a psychiatrist, before finally graduating at 60 from a college in Ireland. But at 70 her husband left her and one of her daughters departed for Australia, never to contact her again. My aunt was able to help others find self-awareness and had attained everything she wanted in her work, yet personal happiness eluded her. The anxiety I sensed in her questioning suggested that she too was looking for something to believe in. I made her a promise I would return in one year's time with the completed film under my arm. But as the months progressed it turned out that I was the one whose faith in my work would be tested. In my second year on *The Navigator* we struck a series of delays, and then disaster. My Jewish aunt held on, but in the following year she died.

THE COLLAPSE

After London I'd headed north to check my medieval mining research, and collect more information. Mines dating from the Middle Ages and unused for hundreds of years can still be found in Cumbria. The photographs I needed were taken by a local enthusiast who crawled along the tiny, wedge-shaped shafts, using candles to show the scale. The technique used to open a new seam underground was ingeniously simple. Miners would heat the rockface by lighting a fire against it, then douse the red hot surface with cold vinegar. If the cave-in wasn't too severe, the dust cleared to expose the seam of ore. I had come across hundreds of engravings depicting these skilled craftsmen digging, sifting, inching along the narrow, triangular shafts. I wondered how these ancestors of ours, with their simple belief in a heaven above and a hell below, would view our century. They were working men, and in my mind I could see their hands. They were my father's hands, ridged and scarred by manual labour, the fingernails permanently twisted by his burns. I had watched those hands all my life, seen them scored with cuts, curled around a shepherd's crook or docking knife, hidden in a leather gauntlet or gesturing eloquently to punctuate one of his stories.

As the story evolved, three images kept appearing, haunting fragments which recurred to shape the narrative: a gauntlet-clad hand, an unknown face behind a blindfold, and a spire. Though the story connections quickly became clear it was some time before I understood where they had sprung from.

Back in Auckland, working on *The Navigator* screenplay in my sixth-floor office, I could see the cathedral spire, dwarfed by mirror-glass buildings. The spire stayed fixed in my mind and made me think of the medieval notion that a witch flying over a church steeple would drop from the sky like a stone. I was reminded too of Chartres Cathedral, whose extraordinary stained glass windows had suggested the colours I wanted for the film. The medieval glaziers, with an eye to lining their pockets, had demanded crushed rubies and the blood of a virgin to achieve the pure, crimson red. But the formula for the rare blue of the Madonna's robe was a secret guarded so zealously that it has been lost forever. If I could recreate the colour of the windows then *The Navigator* would have the look of a medieval vision.

Pre-production commenced in mid-1986. The technicians needed to translate the story into reality arrived and, lit up by their enthusiasm, I watched the film cathedral quickly and painstakingly soar above us, making the dream real. But in the outside world John Maynard was fighting for the film's existence. Film-making is both an act of faith and a gigantic gamble — a punt on an idea taken by financiers, crew, cast and not least by the producer. For a year and a half John had patiently raised the money, but one component of the financial package, dependent on the New Zealand portion, was always missing. He had been negotiating this final deal for three days, when at the last moment unexpected tax changes scared off our major investors. The blow fell as a bulldozer prepared to carve out the terrace of a fourteenth-century mining village in a small extinct volcano on the outskirts of Auckland. Just before it dropped its blade to begin, the phone rang. *The Navigator* finance had fallen through.

John called everyone together at the derelict canteen in the production shed, telling them what had happened. He began, 'This is the worst meeting of my life.' I tried to talk, tried to thank the technicians and builders, but I was too upset to find the words. As often happens when making films, the crew had become like family, and the hardest thing was realising that costume designer Glenys Jackson was still out there hunting enthusiastically for clothing, and didn't know. Twenty-two people had lost their jobs. The sets were chainsawed for firewood. But I was unable to get off the treadmill of expectation and research, and next day dropped over 300 feet by rope into an underground cavern to check out another location.

Back in Auckland we mounted a press campaign to try and change the system that had wrecked our plans but there was little support from other independent film-makers. A week later and against his better judgment, John went to the New Zealand film industry awards, handling the occasion with more grace than I could muster (for a period I hid drunkenly under a table). With surprising tenacity he tried for another two months to refinance the film in New Zealand. Unlike most producers who fly many sails and go with the prevailing wind, John wouldn't abandon course. Angry at what had happened and still stubbornly believing in the screenplay, he took a single suitcase and $25,000 borrowed from a friend, and went to Australia to re-finance the project.

I began to realise that I had to get away from New Zealand, to retreat and reassess. But *The Navigator*, the dream of a medieval world under the cloud of the Black Death, would not let go. Unable to realise the screenplay, the only tangible thing I had left was the story itself, and in my mind it took the form of a manuscript left by a medieval monk, bereft of his faith and bewildered by the times he found himself in.

In the middle of the fourteenth century, a fearsome plague came out of the East. The shadow advanced steadily across Europe, and though no exact records exist, it is believed that over half the population there died. It was the worst epidemic in human history.

 I, Brother John of the Minorite Abbey in Kilkenny, buried the Prior and my thirty-four fellow monks, one by one, sometimes three a day, and was left alone until I could bear it no longer, and with Flynn, my dog, fled.

I reached Dublin, where no death bells tolled, and I believed at first that God had spared the seat of the church in my native Ireland. Soon enough, I discovered the bells were stopped only by city ordinance lest their continuous dolorous ringing plunge the population here yet further into despair. The Archbishop himself was dead of the contagion, and I knew then that even the most reverend authority of divine law was under no protection from the wrath of God, and the death carts came creaking through the streets and I was afraid.

I shipped across the Irish Sea to Holyhead, yet Wales was worse than Ireland, with the valleys scarcely tomb enough to bury the dead, and Flynn's hackles rose again and again, for death's blind head of bone was everywhere. And amongst the living, it is true that the Faith has sometimes receded, for I met men upon the roads who swung smokepots, and who sniffed fragrant herbs and who would tell you that fate is determined not by God's will, but by chance and smokepots, and by seeking the high ground where the fatal vapours drop away.

Therefore, I did get myself a smokepot, and in the winter followed Flynn into the lakeland parishes of Cumbria where we were forced to live upon peapods and bran, for the plague was still so heavily upon their populations that there was no harvest and the wheat lay rotting in the fields, and even the animals that live beneath the surface of the earth came out of the ground disturbed, as if drunk.

I travelled west to the uplands of Cumbria, and though the country here is more bleak, the snowdrifts deeper, the byways more narrow and the villages poor, still there was no abatement in the deadly work of the pestilence. For amidst a snowstorm I came across a broken waysign and a settlement that was now little more than a ghostly outline upon the ground, and grave mounds, and the charred rib of a sunken vessel protruding from the lake alongside. Here Flynn's low growl warned of the approach of a stranger up the same road of our travel, and my hair stood on end lest it was grim death itself that stalked me, for the man's face was hooded and in shadow. Yet he paid

us no heed and whistled a signal across the water.

By then the snowfall had stopped, and I saw a boat put out from the far shore. On land which rose steeply from that shore, I counted sixteen hearths and, by the furnace on the hilltop, I knew it to be a mining village. Then the sun broke from under the cloud, and shone upon this place, and I stood transfixed. I heard the distant cries of children, and a lowing from the cattle pen and, in that yellow light, colonnaded by the thin pillars of smoke which rose from village fires and seemed to join the white earth to the lowering sky, it seemed to me a sanctuary.

The ferryman had but one arm and was called by the name Arno, but I did not glean the name of the other, the gaunt man. He was returning to the village, yet Arno would not take me, except that I stayed on the road west of the village, for the leader there, Searle, forbade anyone to shelter travellers, and except that I paid a penny for passage, and although this was a high price, I paid it.

'It's good luck, meeting a monk,' said Arno. 'Two years ago I ferried a monk like you. It was the monk who told me about the Great Church in the West. The highest church in Christendom, aye, and pilgrims coming from every road to bring stone and wood for its construction, that's what he said.'

We sculled onward in silence for a time.

'You make an offering there — you stop the plague. And so we did it — aye.'

'You reached the church?'

'Well who's to say we didn't eh? Cumbrian copper. That would be a good gift for God's Great Church wouldn't it? We might've done that all right. I think we did.'

'And is there plague in your village?'

'There was!' The ferryman pointed to the silent figure in the bow. 'That one had the shilling in the armpit all right.'

'Why if he is still alive, he should thank God on every breath,' I replied, and the man spoke for the first time in a bitter voice.

'Ah! God, yes. God! Yet I know who to thank too, separate from God!'

Just a year since, I might have shied from the anger in that voice, and advised repentance. Yet when the Brothers died in Kilkenny there was amongst them my one truest friend, Raymond. Upon his death the abyss of my sorrow was so deep and wide I thought to discover there some trace of his immortal soul, or God's reason for taking him. Yet I found nothing, and though it is a fearful thing to admit, my spirit rose in anger and all but closed that mighty door to shut God out. My journey began then, to seek — what? I knew not. A sign perhaps.

'Then you will thank — who?' I asked, but the man said nothing, and stared grimly forward from the bow.

'Cured he was,' said Arno. 'And the village free of the Death these last two years. Ho! Ulf!'

For by then we came up to a landing where a fat man stood ready to catch the rope. Ulf the Fat was the brother of Searle the head man. He made us fast, then went back to place his hand upon a small shrine, and stood smiling. This man was the first I had seen smile in many months. And if I sought some sign in my travels, the boast of a man cured and a village free of the contagion could only serve to whet my curiosity further. I determined more than ever to visit the village, but Arno refused, saying Searle would knock down the walls of any man's hut who gave shelter to a traveller. I succeeded only in buying food, and followed my dog into the dusk on the road west, not knowing where I would sleep.

I was no further than a mile down the road when a messenger came to call me back, saying that the winchman, Old Chrissie, lay dying and, on hearing of a monk passing by, had asked for absolution. By such luck I entered the village, and found that the place, though poor, was wholesome, and if death came, still it was without stink, or black boils, or livid spots, nor with the poison that darts from the eyes of the plague victims to strike down those who would minister to them.

I heard the old man's last confession and he slept, for death, when not hastened by evil, has its own gentleness. Yet there is always a time when the dying man finds himself suddenly on the brink of darkness, and will briefly start up and peer toward the form of what approaches, and cry to his saviour Jesus. So it was with Old Chrissie, as he turned from this world to face the next, and started upright, and saw — what? For his dying word was a name unknown to the Bible, or to the pantheon of Saints, and it was — Griffin!

Towards morning, I laid out the body with the help of the man who was lay priest in the village, though most times he was a hewer in the mine, and his name was Martin. At noon I gave the obsequy, and Searle and Martin lowered the coffin into the ground, and I called for the salvation of the dead man's soul in the name of the Father, and the Son, and the Holy Ghost and, though the fourth name is heresy, still I may be forgiven, for with this utterance I began to pry the village apart from its secret. I called for salvation also in the name of the Griffin, and when I looked up from the Amen, every eye was shining.

I had uttered the name, yet knew nothing, and under Searle's stern gaze, found no one

to tell me more. Then the woman they called Linnet brought me alms of goat's liver and bread, and tripes for Flynn. She sat me in the sun against the wattled wall of her hut, bade me chew slowly, and returned inside.

'The boy Griffin!'

'Yes.'

'He is the younger brother of my husband, Connor. He was barrow boy in the mines. He loaded the bodges.' Thus she whispered to me through the cracks, unseen.

'Griffin had the gift of foresight. When Black Jacob's horse was stolen the boy described a meadow five miles from here, where the horse was found — that was the sort of thing. He was a dreamer, but the gift never set him apart from our people. If aught did, it was his love for Connor, such a love as made my heart melt. Connor was often gone, for ours was the dominant house here, and he was the one to market the copper blooms in the lowland towns, and to bargain on the corn tithes, and the King's tax.

'And Griffin always fretted when Connor was gone. The boy had a small Celtic cross of tin his brother had once brought him from the lowland towns and when Connor was gone too long you'd always see him holding it. And then there was a time when Connor was gone much longer than usual, and the boy began to dream. Why, I

would often find him standing in the lake at dawn, and the dream was always the same. He saw a chasm. He saw the miners underground — Connor, Searle, Ulf, Arno, Martin and himself — in fevered work around a strange engine. They would draw back its iron-tipped ram by windlass and fire it, and the air was full of dust and shouting, and full tilt, again and again they battered at the rock, that they might tunnel at great speed. And they burst out the far side of the earth!'

Now Linnet's story made me smile, for perhaps the boy might predict the location of a horse, yet that gave no credence to a dream of tunnelling through the earth, to fall out into the blackness below. Yet I had seen something more solemn in the eyes of the villagers, and I picked at this tale but gently.

'And what purpose had this strange journey?'

'I asked the boy that very thing, monk, and he knew nothing, except they must beat the evil. It was a journey to beat some terrible evil. It was a fragment without sense. Then a week after the dreaming began, the faggot seller came to our village. He was the first to tell us of the powerful evil on the move. And though it seemed far away, he said, still it was coming closer, hopping foward twenty miles on every full moon.

'So you see, monk, Griffin knew something already. And I kept asking him to tell me more of his dream, but there were just fragments — the chasm, the miners

tunnelling, a glorious city, a spike of molten metal that glowed and pulsed, a black fish, and men roped to a steeple.'

'It was just a dream,' I said softly.

'Aye — a dream. Just a dream,' she said. 'But then the plague was nigh. Connor came back wide-eyed from the terror of the lowlands towns, and all of us here were afraid. We called a meeting. What should we do? Arno spoke of a great church being built in the West, and an offering there stopped the plague — so he was told. The villagers wanted to do that — ah, they wanted it as badly as they wanted to live and not to die. They shouted for it — an expedition to take copper from our mines, to cast a spike for the steeple of God's Great Church. A pilgrimage! What finer tribute could there be? To God, that He might stop the plague. That He might make of our village a sanctuary so the plague would skip right over. Arno called for the expedition, then Martin, then Ulf. Yet — there was no leader. The Hounds of Hell were abroad. Connor would not go out again. Searle neither.

'And then it was too late for a journey. For we heard shouting across the lake and saw the villagers at Gosford staving off the plague boat. They set it afire, but our hearts sank to our feet. For we knew the contagion was loose, and as close as a mile away.

'And the moon rose, full and round, so that our people fell silent. For the moon

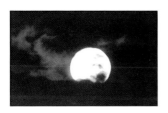

was big and bloated and it was the seal upon our fate. 'Twas the moon would hump the contagion twenty miles on from Gosford that very night like a sack, then let it fall on us. I looked to Griffin. The boy had fallen down, had cried out, in the grip of the moon. And he saw and spoke, his eyes still wide with the dream. The same fragments as before, but now the villagers clustered to him.

'He saw again the chasm. And Arno whispered in sudden awe, he knew of just such a crack in the earth, in an abandoned pit behind the village. Saw again the strange engine, the miners' desperate tunnelling underground, the molten spike, the man upon the steeple. And now we hung upon every word, for if the chasm were true — might not the rest be so? And there was a muttering that rose to a ragged chant. *The journey! The journey!*

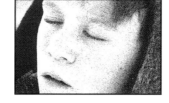

'We understood nothing, the boy neither, but it was like an omen. By then we knew that the desperation of the dream was our own, and the destination — perhaps it was the Great Church.

'An expedition! And Connor, why Connor suddenly stepped forward as leader. Then Arno and Ulf and Martin, all in a rush, and Griffin. Searle doubted the vision, he doubted it deeply, yet it was not just doubt that raised the sweat I saw break out upon his face. For the vision foretold that the men would burst out the far side of the earth.

And who knew what lay there? But the villagers were by now in a whirl of finding ropes, packing copper and shouting instructions, and even Searle was caught up in it. When the party left, he was there beside his brother, Ulf.'

So Linnet told the story and if the mad dream at first had made me smile, it had infused the village, and therefore in this seat in the sun, in this place I could see, and smell, and hear, and touch, this same village, it had infused me. Well, a little, and I was impelled further by a quality in Linnet's voice which gave it soft strength, and a surety I yearned towards, for the quality was belief, but in what? I urged her to go on, but stopped when I saw Searle approaching.

He came down the crooked path towards me, a dark, choleric man, and I saw Linnet was right when she said something lay below the doubt with which Searle had greeted Griffin's story. For he was strong and suspicious, yet beneath you could feel it still — a hub of fear.

'Let the alms we have given you count as a good deed, monk,' he said to me, 'for you are a friend of God, and were a comfort to Chrissie, but now you should not linger here.' And so I was bound to leave the village, yet once beyond its sight on the road west, I sought with a desperate determination on every hill the pit of which Linnet had spoken, and found it at last, and ventured into its darkness, and stumbled on a machine corrupted by decay. Yet did my hands thrill to the shape of a windlass, and rope, and a long smooth shaft, and a tip of iron.

If all else was fancy, still I had entered the jagged portal of the dream, and found the machine, and what else! The chasm! For my foot stumbled upon a torch made of lake reeds and pitch, and as I set it afire, I beheld the terrible crack in the earth. I hurled the torch into this chasm, and it dropped, and dropped, and still it fell on, until the darkness converged upon it, and engulfed it.

'Ho, monk!'

Someone had been watching me! Yet I could not see who, for the darkness had returned, and the stranger made no offer of a name. There was only a following silence, and then Flynn's startled barking clattered around the cavern, and fell away in echoes down the abyss like a harsh and distant carillon, before the voice spoke again.

'Down that road was a journey to make you tremble.'

'I know,' I answered. 'Now tell me of it.'

And this I was told. Down the face of the precipice they clambered, to hitch the rope upon crags and lower the machine, and upon ledges they paused only for breath then

lowered away again, until the crack narrowed and they began to tunnel. And how they tunnelled! The machine bucked and recoiled, but was braced by the miners with shoulders to the helm, and strong arms to the handles and eager hands upon the windlass, and fists to knock away the ratchet release so the long shaft ever leapt forward, and the tip of iron clove the rock, and they battered their way forward amidst dust and sweat and shouts.

With such ferocious speed, four times the length of their rope they tunnelled, nay, perhaps five times, before they struck the last hard rock between them — and the far side of the earth. And the tip of iron broke open a hole, but upon a place so dank and stinking that it made their noses twitch.

By the light of lamps they peered out on such a stream of makewater, and vegetable peelings, and ordure bobbing, that they guessed Griffin's city must indeed lie beyond it, and by the foul density of slops that passed by, that it must indeed be huge. And the boy Griffin was roped, and moved into this tunnel until he found a ladder and pushed up a heavy lid of metal. Though he had already dreamed of it in Cumbria, still nothing had prepared him for what he suddenly beheld.

'I can see it!' he shouted, and his voice came eerily back down the tunnel to the rest of the band. 'The city! The city like — like — all the stars at once!'

The others rushed to see, and one by one their heads popped through the round hole on the nether side of the earth, their faces glowing with wonder.

'It must be God's city,' said Martin. 'There's so much light!'

And indeed, the city had no need of the sun, neither of the moon to shine in it. For the Glory of God did lighten it, and cast a halo of light even into the clouds, and light was scattered as far as the eye could see like burning seeds upon a dark field. And though the miners all still held fast to the rope lest they plummet into the sky, it was Martin who saw about him trees and grass and houses, which had no need of rope, and so did let go, and praised God for his goodness that stuck him there to earth, and all the others.

Searle stared at the stone towers which rose upon the far side of a great harbour, and felt the chill of fear, for the towers bespoke a mighty and unearthly power, yet there was no sign of the Great Church, and therefore he was reluctant to proceed.

'Griffin?' cried Connor, for he would brook no delay, and sought direction from the boy. And Griffin signalled them forward, to the harbour, and the towers beyond.

'We go as the crow flies.' And so they did, and each one held onto the other's tunic, this dark and huddled band running forward into the lustre thrown up by the celestial city, and as suddenly then they came to a halt.

'Griffin! What's that?' asked Connor.

'I — I don't know,' replied the boy, for ahead the light seemed to flow upon the ground like a river, yet was not, for they crept closer and saw the humped form of ten thousand rushing creatures. And each one seemed intent upon a single goal for none deviated a whit from its fellows, but followed the same black path, beaten smooth and wide by the ceaseless passage of those who had gone before, and those who came after. Yet they were not creatures known to mankind, so smooth of flank, and fast, and big, with glowing eyes from which the light shot forth and pierced the night.

'Vermin,' whispered Arno.

'Nay,' said Martin, 'yet perhaps it is all the slain knights of Christendom returning to their long home.'

'Nor that,' said Searle. 'For those things are not God's work.'

'But Searle,' said Ulf, 'if this is God's city, they must be angels.'

'Griffin,' hissed Connor, and the very ground did quake with the terrible passage of what lay before them, 'must we cross that?'

And the boy hung his head, for he knew the answer yet knew also there was danger to overpower any but the most staunch.

'Yes, Con — we must.'

'Then come on!' yelled Connor. 'Band together! Quick! Now go! *Go!*'

And they charged, yet Ulf the Fat stopped dead, and every man was jerked into a tight knot around him.

'Ulf! Move!' bellowed Searle.

'How pretty,' said Ulf, for in truth he saw but the dazzling raiment of angels hovering there, and any man who looked then saw the glittering array which swooped toward him and was blinded and knew neither which way was forward, nor which back, and knew only fear.

'Yaaa-a-a-ah!' screamed Arno, and broke, and ran, whereupon such a cacophony of hoots and screaming broke out as might be made in hell. For these were no angels, but indeed were fiends with bright swords of light, and winking teeth.

'Jesus!' cried Connor, and every hair on his body stood up as that hideous pack engulfed them. 'Run! No! Stop!'

For they came in ranks, as thick and swift as a volley of arrows, and to run was to die, yet the miners could dodge, and jump, and so they did, while around them was a whelming roar, and they did scream instruction to one another, and each man did look out for the other, and pulled him back, or pushed him on.

'Look out! Watch it, Martin.'

'Go! Stop! Another one!'

'Behind you, Con!'

'Whoa! Wait! The gap! *Go!*'

And though Arno had darted through alone, the others were the first to stumble onto the safety of a strip of grass, and Martin sank to his knees and kissed it, then closed his eyes and began to pray. And then Arno staggered in, and began to retch.

'No!' screamed Connor, for now he saw they were but half way, and more came on from an opposing direction and sought to trap them upon this island. 'Keep going!' And he jerked Arno upright, and kicked Martin, and grabbed for Griffin's hand, and shouted at Searle. 'Now! There's a gap! Go!' And they jumped, and hopped, and jerked, and ran for their lives, and fell at last upon the far side of that Styx. But one was missing, and in seeing that, Searle rose, and gripped his pick, and cried in anguish. 'Ulf! Where's Ulf?'

For Ulf had made no ground since his first stop, when those doubters around him had fled, yet he but smiled and held up to the angels the gift he was taking to the Great Church, a little statue of the Holy Virgin. 'Look! Our Lady in wood.'

Then was he buffeted, and spun about with blasts of foul wind, and hounded until his legs would no longer carry him, and fetched up at last on the roadside. But it

was the wrong side, and now Searle saw him there and yelled.

'Wait! I'm coming, good brother!' Then Searle sought to cross, yet straightway came a long, shrill squeal and a demon slithered to a stop, and smoke curled at its feet, and it growled, and began slowly to advance, bellowing. Searle rushed at it, and sank his pick into its head, which had no flesh but was a skull of iron. Then it jumped forward, and bowled Searle head over heels, and when he looked up Connor's restraining hand was upon him.

'Searle — we've got to go.'

'And leave Ulf?'

'No man may cross that twice but he'd be dead, Searle. And we need you.'

'It's fine it's my brother we're leaving behind, isn't it?'

'It's Ulf — or the village, Searle.'

And Searle argued, and raged, but at last he could only shout a promise to his brother who stood bereft upon the far bank, that they would return. And Searle wept, for in his heart he knew the promise to be vain, and so too did all the diminished band that walked away and left Ulf. And now as they journeyed ever deeper into this forbidding land, Searle's distrust of the boy Griffin grew more intense. 'God's city — my arse!' he hissed. For by now they were stealing past row on row of giant houses, and on

the summit of each was a witch's spike, a finial. 'We trusted you, eh? And you give us no warning, do you? Where's your Great Church, Griffin? Where!'

'Leave the boy!' said Connor sharply, for though it was Connor who led their band, and pushed them into the shadows as a demon prowled past, or waved them forward again, still it was to the boy he looked for direction.

To trust the boy, or not; perhaps there was no choice, for if Griffin seemed often as blind and lost as any of them, still it was he alone who might be suddenly jolted — by what? An instinct perhaps. Some echo in this New World of the fragmentary premonitions which had haunted him in Cumbria: the tunnel, the city, the molten spike, the black fish, and the steeple.

And so it was the boy stood stock still, for his nose had caught the faint scent of hot metal, and upon that trail he led them now to a foundry. And therein they met the denizens of the New World, which were not giants, nor witches, nor such breed of men that is sometimes rumoured to inhabit the far-off lands, that have mouths in their stomachs, and travel at great speed on a single foot.

'Jesus!' For so they did greet the miners. And there were three, and each had ten fingers, and two eyes and a nose, and a mouth and though their tongue was strange, yet could each group understand the other if the words were taken slowly. And though

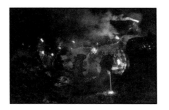

they were men, still their tunics were more finely woven than any on this side of the earth, and their boots had such a stitch and shine as is beyond the skill of any cobbler in the lowland towns.

Yet they were clever too in their trade. For if the miners might dream of a furnace without need of wind up a bald hill to fan it, nor need of a deep charcoal bed to heat it, then here it was, and if they might dream that a furnace needed no stone sump to gather the run-off, but that instead the crucible might be drawn forth direct from the furnace and poured without struggle by a single lever, then here too was that.

And there were machines beyond dreaming, to grind and shape any metal, and the very walls of this foundry were of thin metal, furrowed with amazing exactitude, and from the roof hung lights which had not need of wick nor tallow.

And here the miners found bollards, and bells, and statuary, and it was Martin who found the casting bed for a job still unfinished in the Celestial City.

'Oh yeah,' said the man called Smithy, and he brushed away cobwebs and dust from it. 'We were going to pour that once, but the church ran out of money.'

And Griffin was staring at the casting bed, for impressed upon it was the shape of the spike and its encompassed cross, the exact shape he had seen glowing in his dream, yet it was grey and empty.

'The church is poor?' asked Martin of Smithy.

'Well, like any other business,' said the man. 'If people don't like what you're selling —'

'Selling!' said Martin. 'Yet surely pilgrims have come from every road, just as we have, with gifts for the Great Church?'

'Gifts!' said Smithy, 'Well put it this way. You're probably the first.'

'Aye!' said Connor, for he had watched Griffin's excitement, and knew the boy had brought them another step of the way. 'Cumbrian copper!'

'For God's Great Church!' said Searle, and upended his pack so the copper pigs spilled across the floor.

'For the spike, Smithy!' cried Griffin, tugging at the man, and dancing about with excitement. 'You've got to cast it, you've got to. Please? Cast it — you must!'

'Sshhh, boy,' said Smithy, yet he could not stop smiling, and even as he turned to his two guild workers, the answer to the boy's question was written on his face.

And so the molten spike came true, red and glowing. But at the foundrymen's insistence it was left to cool slowly lest it crack, and Connor paced the foundry yard, pent up and anxious. Again and again his eyes turned to the moon as it passed its zenith, and began its quick slide towards dawn. For at dawn the spike must be raised or their mission fail, and the incubus of contagion hatch in the village. And Connor chafed and fretted and checked their ropes and pulleys that they might be sufficient to do their job, and paced the yard and then upon the instant stood listening intently, and slipped away, and was gone half an hour.

Upon Connor's return the spike was turned from the mould, yet it was still hot enough to blister the skin, and the foundry men gave to Connor leathern gauntlets that he might carry it onward, and bade the miners farewell. And so they set out again, yet at the first bend in the road Arno saw that their band was now increased by one, and went pale, for a white mare stood tethered to a pole there, and Arno knew that it had been stolen by Connor to winch up the spike. And so they went on, with Arno bringing up the rear and shouting most pitifully that he could take no part in an expedition which thieved a horse. And well he might grumble, for the others knew he had lost his right arm as a youth in punishment for horse theft.

Thus they reached the shoreline, already doubtful and anxious, and found now they were without further path to follow except the moonlight across a gulf of dark water. They stopped, and Searle stood over Griffin. 'Now what, boy?'

'We cross water.'

'How?' And all the miners hung over the boy but Connor, who searched the shoreline and found there a boat upturned with oars and rowlocks beneath, and all joined together to tug it to the water but Arno, who was left to lead the horse, and to cast desperate glances over his shoulder, until the others were ready to load the animal on board.

'Ha!' cried Arno, for the felony of theft now had two parts, the horse and the boat, and he saw that one might cancel the other. 'Take a ferryman's word for it, you'll never get a horse that big into a boat this small.'

Yet with Griffin pulling from the front, and Connor and Martin pushing the rump, the horse jumped nimbly aboard, and Searle guided the boat into deeper water, with Arno splashing along behind.

'Oh aye,' shouted Arno. 'And the devil's work always was easy to do, wasn't it!' Yet he clambered on board at last and soon all were lost to wonder, for the great eminences of the city were now but a mile distant, and loomed larger with every passing moment, and were lit from within by serene fires, and cast their reflections in glinting pathways on the ocean. But the moon slid down the western wall of the sky slowly towards dawn and their mission was urgent. Searle bent to the oars, while Connor stood in the bow beside Griffin to discern such landfall as would best serve their purpose, and began to don about himself such tools as would be needed to hoist the spike. And yet of the Great

Church there was no sign.

'I don't like it,' said Searle, casting a look over his shoulder at the two brothers. 'For surely nothing should be higher than a church steeple?'

And then all fell quiet, and though Searle rowed with great strength, they moved but slowly for the weight of their cargo. And more slowly yet did a deepening shadow of evil fall across them, but by such faint increment that they could not exactly know the change, save that their foreboding increased, and seemed to suck all hope from the air, and turn all colour to grey, and sap any speech, and only the horse whinnied uneasily, in fear.

'We should never have stolen that horse,' whispered Arno, for he felt, and they all did but no one quite knew, the approach of the nemesis. 'Griffin,' said Searle softly. 'You should warn us. You must warn us if —'

'Be quiet,' said Connor.

And then it rose up from the deep, and a giant fin cleft the water, then a black body that sundered the ocean as far as the eye could see, and it rose up with a roar, water streaming from its flanks, and such was its power to harrow up the soul, no man in that tiny boat looked at it further lest he be turned to stone, or have his wits blown away.

Only the boy looked, and saw it was vast, and swollen with the evil in it, and knew that if plague came upon the earth it was monsters as huge and sleek as this would bring it, and Griffin screamed, 'Con!'

Connor turned, and shielded his face to see. 'Griffin! It is death!' And Griffin's eyes had gone black with fear. 'I — I didn't see that! How could I have seen that!'

With barely a ripple the great black nose slide towards them, and now only Connor moved, and picked up his shovel, and as the beast came up behind, so he moved to meet it at the back of the boat, and raised his weapon higher as it closed upon them, and smote it. In that moment the creature's fluke struck the back of the boat, knocking Connor off balance so he fell spreadeagled across it and was swept away. Griffin stood rooted to the spot as he saw his brother flail desperately against the mighty flank, and then saw him claw his way onto the black nose, and stand upright, hands outstretched and helpless, and saw him scream yet no sound came. And Griffin stood transfixed, yet in that moment the eyes of the two brothers met, and Griffin's love flew to his brother. Ah, that the gaze was an arrow, and that the arrow bore a rope to carry Connor back, but naught could stop that dreadful passage, and even as the boy watched his brother was borne ever further into the night, away and away. Then the

spell broke.

'Kill it!' screamed Griffin, for the monster's long flank still slid alongside the boat, and every passing yard of that malign body bore Connor away, and the terror of loss gripped the boy so that he cast about him for some way to stop the creature and found a gaff and raised it high above his head, and lunged. And with all his might Griffin drove the weapon into the side of the beast, yet it glanced with impunity off that terrible hide, and the boy lunged again but the gaff twisted in his grasp and the cruel hook of it tore his hand. Yet the heat of battle was upon him now and he paused only to cast around the boat for a new weapon and to rouse the others to fight.

Then Searle rose up and swung an oar with such force against the beast that the blade shattered, and as Griffin flung bottles to burst upon the enemy, Searle cursed it with hoarse cries, and stabbed into it again and again, and Martin stood close up against the sliding wall of it, and held up his arms clenched to the shape of our Saviour's cross, and chanted at the top of his voice the pig Latin. 'Pater noster! Qui est in Coelis!'

'Get it!' shouted Arno, and from beneath the stamping hooves of the horse he lugged out the spike and braced it upon his stump ready for the charge. 'You hell-bent lump of dung!'

'No!' Searle turned, and saw the spike poised and ready to harpoon the creature, 'Not that! Arno — put it down! Drop it!' For already the swart beast had slid by, and all the miners stood drooped and panting, and Griffin had begun to cry and Searle took charge, grasping Arno's arm.

'For we may lose Ulf,' said Searle, and looked to the wailing boy in the bow, 'aye, and we may have lost Connor. Yet we may not lose the spike, or the village itself will perish.'

And the two men made to lay the spike down upon the keel, yet saw the boat was awash with water, and more gushed in through a hole in the stern.

'We're sinking!' screamed Arno. 'Mother of God! Sancta Maria, not in the ocean deep! I can't swim!' And in those wild moments, even the loss of Connor was forgotten, for the boat was likely to founder; yet Searle gave swift orders.

'Martin! Plug that leak. Use your fist — and these rags!'

'Arno! Take the good oar. Scull us in! Fast!'

And Searle bailed furiously, and shot a glance from under his dark and desperate brow to the small figure who sat in the bow. 'And you! Is it the last church in Hell you're taking us to, boy? And what happens now? Tell us! Tell us!' Yet Griffin made no reply but sat hunched in the bow, his punctured hand clenched upon the rag to staunch the bleeding of the gaff wound, bereft of Connor, sobbing and sobbing, and Searle the leader now, whose voice battered him, demanding direction.

'Tell us what happens, damn you. The dream! The dream, Griffin!'

Yet the dream had come only in Cumbria, and had come unbidden, as a gift of the mind, and to seek it from Griffin was vain. Vain perhaps, but in Cumbria it had come to the boy as he stood surrounded by water under a bright moon, and it had come to a boy distraught for his brother. And so it was now, for Griffin fell into a swoon. And he saw again the steeple, and upon it now saw men climbing as the spike was hoist beside them. He saw a cowled figure whose face was in shadow climb the ladder, rung over rung. And one of the man's hands wore a gauntlet, and one was bare, hand over hand up the ladder . . . and then those hands lost grip . . .

And with that, Griffin screamed and awoke from his dream.

'Griffin!' said Searle. 'What?'

'He fell!' whispered the boy. 'He fell! One of us dies at the cathedral.'

In that moment Arno stopped his sculling, and Martin looked round in fear from his plugging of the splintered stern, and Searle straightened and threw down the bailer with a splash, and crossed swiftly to the boy and stood above him. 'Who dies?'

'Hand over hand,' said Griffin, and his eyes were still black and half in dream, 'and then — he fell.'

'Ah,' cried Arno, and began to scull, and wagged his stump in the air, 'if it's hand over hand — it's not me!'

And Searle whirled back upon Griffin.

'Tell us!' And Searle did shake the boy. '*Who?*'

'I — I don't know.'

'Don't know! It's me isn't it? *Me!* Aye, the end for me. Oh yes. I've watched them all picked away. My wife in childbirth — picked away. The child she died for. My mother. Then Ulf —'

'I want Connor!' screamed Griffin. 'I want my brother back!'

And while Searle stood over him, his fists knotted in rage and fear, Griffin pulled from his pocket the little Celtic cross that Connor had once given him, and sat huddled in the bow, stroking it. And then Arno gave an excited cry.

'What's that? Look! Look!'

For every yard of progress toward the shore now opened up new depths and distances within the city, and shyly into sight crept a long slim cone, which seemed to yearn heavenward even amongst the grim and overbearing towers which surrounded it on all sides.

'The steeple!' cried Martin.

'The Great Church!' croaked Arno.

And all craned to see but Griffin, for he was still combing in his mind the premonition of moments before, certain of some clue embedded there, yet not knowing what, and he saw again the hands — the gauntlet!

'No!' whispered the boy. For only one of their band wore gauntlets, and in that moment he knew that his brother did not die upon the back of the seabeast, but might yet die on the steeple, and he rose up, and yelled.

'It's Connor! Connor is the one who falls!'

And Griffin knew then he must fly to the steeple to save his brother, who did not know his death was foretold. And he knew that Searle's suspicion and the waterlogged boat would only slow him, and quick as a flash he leaped for the gunwale, and dived overboard, and struck out for the shore. And Searle stared after him, flabbergasted.

'The boy! We're blind without the boy!' And with a curse, he swung up onto the horse, and jumped it over the side, for Griffin must not escape, and Martin and Arno were left to beach the boat, and bring on the spike.

And indeed, Connor had been carried in to the city by the sea monster, and did jump off upon a pier and sighted the Great Church, and ran to it, and had already climbed the steeple upon a ladder affixed to it, and was even now lashing trusses and a pulley to its pinnacle, and with desperate strokes, for the first blush of the approaching dawn was upon the eastern sky.

Only when that top was made secure did he look up, and out, and was seized by despair, for upon the harbour was no sign of his fellows who bore the spike. He saw the city was a vast maze and he knew his band might never reach their goal. And he shouted, this tiny figure perched black upon a spire with the lightening sky behind, a useless sound in the vastness of this place. Then he remembered a signal that was within reach if he but descended the ladder, and was more potent than any human voice to sound across the city, for it was the sound of God.

Griffin was lost. He ran pell-mell into the city, but the road branched and forked and at every turn he was hemmed about as by a thicket, and could see no steeple, nor choose one road from another except that once he heard a chuckle, and an iron skull peeped around a corner, eyes flashing, and he veered away and did not look back

except once to see men feeding it, with buckets. And he ran, and stopped, and ran on ever deeper into the rifts and chasms of the great city and ever deeper into despair. And about him now the lights rose up to the sky as if countless ranks of pure souls stood sentinel on the mighty cliffs, and before him a legion of others floated and winked and waved their lights, and the boy felt himself running headlong into the great storm of the *dies irae*, the day of wrath, where every soul is lost amongst the millions of the dead, and the greater the glare, the more does every feature fade, and every trait grow dim. And he stopped, helpless.

'Connor! Con!' And there was no reply. Yet around a distant corner now galloped Searle on the horse, and Griffin ducked away into an alley. And there he stopped, aghast, for perhaps Searle was right and this place was indeed Hell, and if all punishment visited on sinners be suited to their sin, then those who spoke to him now were gossips and prattlers for their heads had been cut off and put in boxes, yet they talked on and did not stop even as the boy shouted his question. 'Where's the cathedral?'

Yet they nodded and smiled, and talked on, and Griffin turned and saw Searle, and then he screamed for the horror of this world and burst into tears, and in that moment, rolling through the streets came the sound of the church bell.

'Griffin! Listen!' said Searle, and put a strong arm around the boy. And as fast as hope had wilted, so now did it spring up again, and the boy stood, twitching, to locate the sound. Yet the city was full of echo, and the sound rolled down streets, and changed course, and rolled back on itself. And towards them now ran Arno and Martin, one on either side of the spike, and each pointing in high excitement.

'You hear that?' panted Arno. 'That'll be the Great Church. This way!'

'No!' Martin called. 'Over here!'

'Come back, you turnips!' shouted Searle. 'It's the boy will bring us.'

And Griffin's head swivelled, yet the sound seemed without source. It echoed all around, and the boy could gain purchase on naught but the lights which taunted and mocked, and flashed all about, and he put a hand to his brow.

'It — it's like I see too much! Searle! Black my eyes — quick. Blindfold me.'

So the boy was blindfold that did move forward and stop on every corner, his head cocked first this way, then that, yet he did lead Arno and Martin and Searle and the horse through the mingle-mangle of streets to the Great Church. There Searle stripped the blindfold away, and by then Connor was back at the top of the steeple, and Griffin saw him there, and cried out.

'Connor! Don't move!'

The boy ran for the great doors, with Searle close behind. He ran with pounding feet up the great spiral stairs of stone, and past the belfry where the great bell still hummed.

Connor had heard the boy's cry and looked down from that fearful height, and his head sank with relief against the ladder, that the spike was brought to its destination and there might still be time enough. But the paling sky made every movement urgent, and turned him back to his work.

With feverish hands he yanked rope through the pulley, and leaned way out to heave the heavy coil of rope so it might fall without hindrance to the eager hands of Arno and Martin far below. And as he threw the heavy coil, his single handhold upon the steeple gave way. In that moment, Connor fell headlong and screaming down the pitiless roof. Yet did the widening slope of the steeple intersect Connor's fall so that his frantic hands again touched the ladder, gripped it, and his plunging body swung back with a crash against the ladder. And the rung that turned his fall snapped then, and he plummeted on, arms flailing wildly for a handhold, and found it, and hung finally upon the edge of the abyss on a single cracking rung.

Then far below Arno and Martin saw falling through the air, not

Connor, but a shower of broken wood, and a single gauntlet, wrenched from Connor's hand, spinning through the air to fall at their feet.

And now Griffin burst through the trapdoor at the base of the steeple, and far below him saw the white faces of those shocked and silent witnesses to Connor's near fatal plunge. And high above him hung his brother.

'Con!' screamed Griffin. 'Wait!'

Yet there could be no pause. For down in the courtyard, Arno now bound the horse stem to stern with the pulley rope and led the mare back, to hoist the spike smoothly into the air. Connor saw it come, and high upon his perilous perch he saw more clearly than any man the light of dawn arrayed upon the eastern horizon, and he saw that in minutes, unless there was a man at the steepletop to guide the spike home, Sol's fiery orb would crack the eastern horizon, and their mission fail.

So that Connor did not wait, but hauled himself upward again, and one hand upon the ladder was bare, and the other gloved.

'Wait!' Griffin's thin cry rang out below, but to no avail, and he set foot upon the ladder and climbed swiftly after his brother. Then his punctured hand began to bleed but still he came on, and above him Connor's climb was suddenly halted. So that the boy reached him at last, panting, and blurted his warning.

'Con! It's not safe for you!'

Then brother trembled against brother as Connor put a strong arm around Griffin in that dizzy place.

'It's safe for no one, Griffin. The spike not raised — still not! And look!'

Then Griffin saw that his brother's climb was halted by the missing rungs knocked away by Connor's fall, and the ladder could be scaled by no man. Yet he saw the gap was such that he might use his brother's shoulder as a step, and reach across it. And the boy hardly paused.

'Lift me.'

'Griffin! Can you do it?'

'Yes.'

And Griffin clambered onto Connor's shoulders and strained towards the next rung, but his hand was slippery with blood.

'Griffin! You'll not get good grip with that hand. Here!'

From below him Connor held up the leathern gauntlet, and the boy reached down and drove his hand inside it, and straightened, looked out across the world, and reached up and gripped the ladder, and began to climb. He saw now his own hands upon the rungs, and deep inside himself his soul shivered, for one hand was gloved

140

and the other bare. But he climbed on, and silently beside him rose the spike — to the steepletop, and there, as if in fulfilment of the dream, the cowled figure which was himself swung the spike around by main force. And as the sun cracked the eastern horizon and a bolt of light darted across the dark city, Griffin sank the spike into its waiting socket. Far below him, he heard the cheers of his mining band, and in a sudden ecstasy of triumph raised his fist to the sky. And then a black wing passed across his mind, his hand upon the spike lost grip, and the gauntlet fell away. The boy pitched outwards from the steepletop, and tumbled toward the street below.

'Well monk,' said the voice from the dark cavern. 'Such is our story, and so it ends.'

And I said nothing, but sat awhile in darkness, stroking Flynn, and my eyes were pricked by tears. For though I should be cautious of this tale, it had seemed to touch strange verities, and its ending was keen with pain. And then came the sparking of flint and the storyteller lit his torch, so that I saw before me the same gaunt man of yesterday, with his face still cowled, and his visage grim, and the whole of him pinched upon some secret trouble. I stared at him awhile. 'You are Connor,' I said.

'Yes, monk.'

'And most surely then, you did not abandon the boy's body in that place, but carried back his brave bones to the village?'

Then did Connor laugh, and it was no pretty sound, that stopped as suddenly as it began, and he held me with his piercing gaze.

'Monk, you know nothing. He brought himself back, for even as he began to fall he screamed, and awoke from his dream.'

'Then you never left the cave,' I said. 'It was just a dream.' And in truth the thought made me happy, for it seemed better that the monsters of the tale should have life only in some eldritch imagination, and better that the boy should live.

'Just a dream? No!' cried Connor, and he seized my habit, and thrust his face to mine. 'The boy was a seer! His spirit was elsewhere that night, and it was no realm of dream, but a place — such a place. For how else did he hold us in such thrall throughout that terrible night? He saw! And he spoke what he saw! And it was vivid, and real and deadly!'

Then Connor's passion subsided, and he grew quiet, and the brokenness returned, and he spoke softly.

'The story does not finish there. If you would know it all, you would know my shame, and such betrayal of the boy's faith in me that torments me to this day.'

I went to him, and put a hand on each of his shaking shoulders, and looked at him though his eyes were downcast. 'Tell me,' I said.

When the boy started awake from his dream the sun had just arisen, and the bell of the village had begun distantly to ring. And away from that cavern, and towards that joyous ringing the men trudged, and found the villagers swarming towards them with the glad cries of reunion, and the breathless news that no one had fallen ill. And all of the band were pressed for detail of their journey, and praised as heroes, and Griffin the boldest of them. The pent-up fear of the night now turned to joy that the moon had sunk, and the sun arisen, and no contagion had hatched, and the joy turned to wonder that the dream journey might indeed be a sign that they were to be kept safe.

And even Searle thought perhaps it was so, and the pipers were roused to play, and the villagers gathered to dance upon the smelting ground.

Griffin danced with the rest, believing in his dream, and danced the wilder in the fling that he might forget all but the dream's wonderful promise of salvation. And then he staggered, and sneezed, and felt under his arms the little lumps, like eggs, and then did the events of the night stand before him in stark array, and he saw their terrible pattern, and he saw their cause, and looked about him — for Connor.

The boy had contracted the Death, and it was from his brother, and in that moment he knew it, and dashed to where Connor stood at the lake shore, and stripped away his tippet, and saw there upon his brother's neck the plague scars.

'Con! You knew! All the time you were sick! And you knew!' Connor could say nothing.

'How could you have come back?' And he who had never shouted at his brother shouted now with such mortal hurt as would haunt Connor forever. For Connor knew who had picked the boy up and swung him around for joy upon his return from the lowland towns. And Connor knew who had hastened Griffin ever onwards upon his dream journey. And worse than that, Connor knew that the black boils upon his neck were drying up and he would get well, yet now that Death was upon Griffin. And he who had been so high in his brother's esteem now fell so low, and could do naught but appeal to the boy, that he might salvage a little of Griffin's respect.

'Griffin. It's true I felt the sweat upon me when I returned from the lowland towns. I — dismissed it as of no consequence. And I swear I did not know for sure . . . not until your story was hours old . . . and the black evil rose from the depths. It was Death! And it bore me away.'

And by now, all that band which had made the dream journey were gathered about, and Connor appealed to them all.

'Then it was I felt upon my neck . . . ugh! The boils. And backed away from you all, lest by poisonous breath or gaze I condemn you. I kept my distance. I believed I should die, yet Griffin — without knowing, still he sensed my mortal danger, and in his vision he told my story and kept my hope alive, and fought to save me. To save us all!'

'And yet,' said Searle, and the fear was back in his voice, 'if the infection's loose . . .'

'No!' said Griffin. 'In the dream one dies — only one.'

And then it was that Linnet, in sudden knowledge that it was the boy who died, started forward to gather him up.

'No!' said the boy. 'For the village is safe, but I must go alone.'

And he pulled from his pocket the tin cross, and kept his gaze upon it, and backed away, and stopped, and they saw his eyes were already dark with the dream.

'It seems to shimmer, Con! And it is deep, deep in the water.'

'He died that same day, monk,' said Connor. 'And I bound the Celtic cross to the coffin

by its leathern strap, for it was a thing he much treasured, and it trailed away beneath the lake water as I pushed the coffin out. I saw it shimmer, monk! And I knew then he was arisen, and gone, and bade him . . . Godspeed.'

And whether it was panic or quest which had driven me upon strange roads far from Kilkenny, it seemed now, by the hearing of this tale, much abated. For in truth I who fled the abbey had lost my faith, but now had uncovered a miracle that seemed to yield hope, though whether of the Deity or some stranger force was moot, for if miracle it be, it was most savage.

So I foresook the road west, and walked back with my dog and the silent Connor to the village, then on down the track to the lake. And while I awaited passage, I spoke to Ulf the Fat, who stood beside the jetty, his hand still upon the shrine.

'So, Ulf,' and I teased him a little. 'You got stuck at the black highroad.'

'Aye,' he replied, and looked glum, yet his smile was soon back. For he was broken-hearted too that night in the cavern, but at daybreak, on the walk back to the village, Griffin had recounted the rest of Ulf's story.

'Pluck,' said Ulf. 'Real pluck, that's what he said I had. I went under the black

highroad you see. Long after everyone was gone I dug through, and crawled up the hill on the other side. Right to the top. And I held up the Little Virgin. I showed her the lights of the Celestial City. I did that much, monk. Griffin said so.'

Then Ulf took my hand and placed it upon the shrine, saying it was luck for any traveller, and I saw therein a lock of hair, and the fingernail parings of some small saint, and knew it was no saint hallowed by the church.

By then Arno was ready at the oar to row me back across the lake, and I took my leave, but my gaze was ever back over my shoulder at the village, which seemed indeed a place apart from the world to which I was returning. The further from Griffin's village I travel, the further that glow of a supernal will does recede into darkness, for in the experience of all who have faced the contagion, it skips over no place for long, and if it passes by, either not affecting the people of a place or touching them in indifferent manner, still at a later time it always comes back. And I have known doubt, yet hold to that tiny light in a world darkened by the Evil One. And any who cherish hope would do well to visit the village in the years ahead to bear witness that it was neither by luck, nor chance, nor smokepot that the village was vouchsafed its particular sanctity, but by some boon granted a young boy, in realms of terror, at a terrible cost. So it is with truth.

And I await passage to Ireland, yet this very day a magpie stood upon my windowsill, and this night, beyond the window of my inn, there is a star in the horn of the moon. Such omens are not good. Death's snare is all around, the charnel crews come through the streets of Holyhead, and my ship is unaccountably delayed.

So it is that I, Brother John of Kilkenny, writing as if among the dead, have put down what I have heard and verified. And that the writing may not perish with the scribe, and the work fail with the labourer, I add parchment to continue it, if by chance anyone may be left in the future, and any child of Adam may escape the pestilence and aid the work thus commenced.

It seems likely the monk died at Holyhead. The manuscript was found in the crypt of a parish church there, suggesting he travelled no further than the port town. It had lain unread for centuries. No subsequent writing was appended to it, and the strange tale was without influence on church history.

I moved to Australia, feeling as bitter and frustrated as when I first left home. I realised I couldn't work in New Zealand, and staying would constantly remind me of my failure.

Sydney revitalised me. I had last seen Kings Cross 10 years before. I stayed in a storage room filled with old scripts and letters in the flat of an actor friend, setting up my office between the filing boxes and spare bed, like a character out of Kafka. All the time I clung to my normal working routine, concentrating on the film. The belief that it could be made wasn't totally baseless, as John thought it possible for the film to be the first Australian-New Zealand co-production. Gradually we grew more confident, but there was always the worry that again the financial deal would collapse. It finally came through, but it was late and put us behind schedule. The money raised was really not enough, but as there was no chance of raising any more we decided to go ahead, shooting on a schedule that was clearly too tight.

I started to search again for the key people — the cameramen, the designer and the actors. There was another long search through schools, for a scrawny, tough-looking boy to play the lead. I could imagine the working conditions of the time, when they would shove a kid like Griffin down a mine shaft and expect to get a day's work out of him. I wanted a kid you would believe was equal to this, and eventually I found Hamish McFarlane.

We found Ulf the Fat working for the city council in the Auckland sewers. Noel Appleby was shy during the audition and he had no film experience, but he *was* the character. He was 70 pounds overweight, suffered from emphysema, and had been warned by his doctor that he could die before the picture was finished. Noel said the film was the most important thing in his life and he held an unshakeable belief in it, yet found it strange that the others took it all so seriously. Despite problems remembering his lines he turned out to be a natural actor, explaining to me in his straightforward way, 'I'm the kind of ordinary bloke who always cries at funerals and laughs at weddings.'

I found Connor in New York, the city where I had begun the screenplay. The casting director in London mentioned an actor she'd seen in an off-Broadway play, coincidentally an actor I knew. Watching his audition tape it was obvious Bruce Lyons was right for the part.

Ironically he was married to one of my co-writers, Kely Lyons, who'd always conceived of him as Connor, and I could picture her privately crowing at the choice I'd made. Bruce brought to the film an almost religious intensity, but he was so thin that I wondered if he was starving into character. His costume gave him the look of the Grim Reaper, but the burning gaze was all his own. Although he clearly regarded the film as a series of personal tests, at the outset I didn't realise that it would also become this for me.

The first location was Lake Harris, a glacial lake in the Southern Alps of New Zealand, over 3000 feet above sea-level, which was to be used as the landscape of the miners' village. I set my heart on the lake because it reminded me of Cumbria, though it was starker and more dramatic than the English landscape. I knew the film needed a strong opening and closing and that in purely financial terms the expense of shooting here would prove worth it on the screen. We soon discovered that by the scheduled starting date the lake would be frozen over, making it impossible to film there, so the filming had to be brought forward by several weeks.

This decision put unwanted pressure on everyone. Glenys Jackson, our costume designer, was on a seemingly impossible schedule to produce the mass of medieval garb needed for the opening scenes. Each piece had to be hand-dyed and partially hand-sewn.

The art department had a similar problem. There were hundreds of designs for every possible prop item: adzes, picks, torches, lamps, shovels, even 12 madonna icons among the masses of research I'd prepared, all needing to be examined in relation to the equipment that best suited each character and best furnished different parts of the set. Although much of this would have been left up to Sally Campbell, the production designer, my concern about detail meant the need for laborious comparison and consultation. Sally (a flamboyant Sydneysider with bright red hair, whose one weakness was an emergency red '59 Plymouth with four-foot chrome fins which attracted marriage proposals at traffic lights) found herself falling even further behind. Waiting on my decisions and wondering whether she should just press on, she knew that if she did so I would very likely ask for things to be re-done, sometimes more than once. It was exasperating her and the art department, which was already working impossible hours largely out of loyalty to her. Finally Sally delivered an ultimatum: I had to make my mind up more quickly or she and the art director would quit. She stayed and we sorted things out.

And so, almost exactly a year after the first financing collapsed, we arrived at Lake Harris. Inwardly I knew as we prepared to meet the mountain that we were also preparing to meet ourselves.

The 23 of us, cast and crew (including a pregnant actress and three children), were apprehensive and excited. Although the crew were rigged out with Antarctic clothing some of them were worried about the possibility of frostbite in these conditions. But Lake Harris was more than a difficult location. It was another world. Untouched and silent, the virgin snow, the mist and fog rising out of the lake and creeping towards the mountain made our presence seem insignificant, even bizarre.

It became a running joke with the crew that I chose difficult locations deliberately: 'Vincent found a new location today, but we're not using it. You can get there by road.'

At Lake Harris it took two hours to get the gear in and set up a base camp, because everything and everybody had to be lifted in by helicopter. A four-foot 59-year-old with curvature of the spine was to play the village midwife. Dressed in long-johns, trousers, three dresses, bindings, plastic bags and large boots, she leaped from the cockpit, heart in her mouth, and swiftly sank up to her head in the snow.

We all had our private fears. Noel Appleby was afraid he would find the alpine location physically too tough, saying, 'Short legs and deep snow, thin air and a fat man don't go together.' My concern was to do with lack of time. Even if we had no problems

with the weather, we could only afford to film for two days on the mountain, making it impossible to get all the shots I needed.

Each evening the helicopters flew in early to ensure they could get everyone out before dark. On one side of the mountain the valleys were filled with mist. If it drifted over the ridge to where we were filming, it would be impossible to get the helicopters in or out. Some of us were barely fit enough to forge the narrow path out on foot to the emergency hut part way down the mountain, where John Maynard kept a constant check on the weather to make sure we were not stranded.

The boy Hamish who played Griffin had fought fiercely for the part, but he was worried that when the cameras actually rolled he might dry up. On only his second day of filming he had to face his hardest scene.

At 4.45 in the afternoon we had our first and last chance to film the story's final climactic scene. Griffin confronts Connor. He is aware that his brother, the person he loves most in the world, has betrayed him by returning to the village with the plague. Connor has infected him — and then as Griffin realises that his dream foretells his own death, his voice begins to crack. In that instant the helicopters arrived too early. The sound boomed off the peaks and their twentieth century din hit us as they slowly circled over the lip of the ridge. In my miner's cassock (I was doubling as an extra) all

I could do was yell impotently at the sky. The film's most important sequence seemed ruined.

To Bruce the helicopters hovering overhead, whipping snow across his face, provided the key to his character's climactic confrontation. In replying to his brother's question, 'Why did you do this?', it seemed to him that in this world of elements larger than man, he had to answer to God.

After the cold and blinding light of the Southern Alps, we set up in an old foundry to film the Celtic cross being cast for the cathedral. Workers toiled in unbearable heat, amid rivulets of molten slag coagulating on the earthen floor. Again I was pressed for time and, stripped to my waist, shouting to actors who could not hear me above the roar of the furnace, I could only watch as the bearlike figure of Marshall Napier, in the role of Searle, poured molten metal from the crucible. Suddenly I saw someone jump at him and violently shake him about the shoulders. Someone else threw a bucket of water over him. A spark had caught in the open weave of his costume, setting it alight.

The incident unnerved me. I worried about the safety of the actors during the rest of the filming and that night, in a disturbed sleep, I dreamt I was in a medieval cathedral. There was lightning and I was squeezing past kneeling monks. A hail of hot tiles fell from above and there was panic as the arches caved in. The vast lead-lined ceiling became a scarlet canopy, showering molten metal on those cowering below. Some burning metal dropped on my foot, searing a hole clean through the bone.

We were shooting scenes which often seemed more dream-like than real. A burning arrow arched towards a medieval boat, then another, igniting the sails. The canvas flared, falling in threads of flame which faded into wispy grey fragments before landing on the extras cast as refugees huddling in the stern. Then ghostly figures from the film crew waded out to bring these other apparitions ashore.

Anachronisms were everywhere, and always startling. Up on the hill was a tent filled with 60-odd medievals drinking soup and chatting away, their faces scarred with hideous buboes (plague tumours that were the result of long experimentation with rice bubbles). Away from the tent, down in the bitter cold, the props people were unloading a truck of squealing pigs. Another 30 or so extras on the medieval vessel were being coated with fire gel. I joined a group of extras at the side of the lake practising with

12-foot cavalry pikes, drilling them until they could form a phalanx, raise their pikes in unison and charge the imaginary enemy. The common purpose of all these chimeric activities was our biggest scene. It was also the scene with the greatest potential for disaster and rehearsals lasted several days, until everyone knew exactly what to do.

The villagers attacked the plague-ridden refugees, wading through the water, their staves smashing the boat. The staves got heavier with each attack and the costumes stiffened with the cold. Christine, the second assistant, tried to cheer up the waterlogged medievals by telling them they should pee in their wet-suits to keep warm, while at the same time leading them in a clumsy parody of an aerobics class. The stunt woman, who was supposed to leap from the boat with hair ablaze, tearing off her burning clothes as she plunged into the water, kept having trouble igniting her wig. She had to repeat the stunt three times before wading ashore cold and thoroughly wet. Her footage was never used.

Like most films, this one had a will of its own. I'd begun to feel that it had become like some giant infernal machine in which I was a small cog, able to tilt its direction but unable to change its course. Six weeks into the shoot, the long nights were taking their toll.

We were shooting in bitter weather in a disused quarry near Auckland airport.

The children were the only ones not moaning about the cold and rough, scoria-covered ground. The youngest extra, a four-year-old with a face like a ruddy Botticelli angel, remained cheerful even when he was dragged over the sloping edge of the quarry behind a wayward deerhound. Everyone else was tired and there were rumblings of discontent, exasperation about organisational hitches and a growing feeling that things were becoming inefficient. Finally the crew held a meeting in the quarry to discuss it all. It was a sort of kangaroo court in a Greek amphitheatre, as accusations and criticisms were flung across the arena. I sat in the background through all of it, unclear as to whether it was a lack of organisation, our limited budget or simply my way of working that was causing dissatisfaction. If it was the latter then I hoped the completed film would be my vindication. Despite the grumblings, the group never wavered in its commitment, although weeks of night shoots under difficult conditions had worn us all down.

During all this my parents arrived on the set, taking it all in their stride, my father chatting to one of the pretty extras (my mother said you could always tell when he was talking on the phone to a woman because his voice dropped to a dulcet tone) in the late afternoon sun. My mother enjoyed the makeshift tents and

canteens because they reminded her of the sense of community, the camaraderie and the happiness she'd felt in the army.

While my mother was thinking of the past, Hamish was reeling with joy on the black hill, then stopping still as he realised the tragedy of his predicament. He whispered the word 'Death', and for that instant, that brief moment illuminating the story, everyone was reminded of the purpose of the film. Even the more sceptical members of the crew seemed moved, despite their fatigue. This boy Hamish sometimes seemed the most adult of us all. Eleven years old and always enthusiastic, he saw the whole thing as an adventure, wanting to know how everything worked: the helicopters, the cameras, the sound equipment, the lighting. He would become so caught up we'd have to force him to go home before the end of each night's filming.

Our main set was the three-story cathedral spire, and to me it had always seemed symbolic of our re-kindled enthusiasm, tangible evidence that the film was being made at last. The spire had been the first set to be chopped up after the collapse of the initial production, and it had been re-built to stand taller and more complete, towering over everything else. During a production meeting in the last weeks of the shoot, we heard a loud noise, like a thunderclap. 'My God, what was that?' I thought. A few minutes later the art director, pale-faced, came in and whispered something in Sally Campbell's ear.

She smiled brightly and said calmly, 'I'll check on that later.' Half an hour passed before she tapped me on the shoulder. 'Darling,' she said, 'that wasn't thunder resounding in your ear — our main set just crashed to the ground.' The spire smashed into thousands of pieces, and there was nothing to do but go on working, filming final close-ups against the fragments.

I suppose it was curiously appropriate that I was shooting pieces — I always see the close-ups, the details, before the overall pattern. By looking down the wrong end of the telescope, I failed to notice that sets weren't the only thing crashing behind me. There was a memo from Sally: 'Would you fuckwits get your act together so that the art department can do their job?' It made the point with a humour that barely masked her all too genuine exasperation. She had met constant changes in schedules, made literally hundreds of changes to her sets, and had accommodated my pickiest demands

with amiability and wit. But now, instead of giving her usual stroppy retort when I criticised one of the sets, she went silent. It was obvious by the look on her face that she was at the end of her tether. For a week she was stricken by a virus that insidiously infected us all.

We shot the scenes involving our leviathan, a

100-foot submarine, at a former sewage pond in South Auckland. Again it was freezing and almost every night it rained. The small pond, known to everyone as 'the bullshit lake', stank. In the early morning vapour rose from it like a weird yellow mist. Several crew members fell ill, their suffering usually mild but sometimes taking a severe form that produced hallucinations and vomiting. Bruce, on the edge of delirium and despair from the long nights and constant waiting, began to speak melodramatically of a plague among us, whispering cryptically, 'There is a dark underbelly to this film; they are trying to kill us.' Rumours of blood poisoning and typhoid spread. The sickness brought the already tired crew to the verge of paranoia, blaming the placement of the Portaloo, the residue of effluent and even the ducks on the water for their illness. Glenys came down with the virus, then John, who returned to the set looking as tired and gaunt as a haunted medieval. The location manager and the nurse argued over the laboratory tests for the water. It had been tested before we arrived and more tests showed the water still free of effluent, yet the suspicion remained.

The virus, a vicious flu, struck me the following week. I had a feverish nightmare in which I was back at the bullshit lake and in order to get the shots to complete the film

I had to bail out the whole pond. Every three or four seconds a wave of nausea hit me. I sat up in bed and retched, and every time I retched I was convinced in my nightmare that I was draining the lagoon of rancid water, mouthful by mouthful, faster and faster; a sorcerer's apprentice, rushing to vomit up the entire contents of the lake. In my delirious state old poisons welled up inside me, like my desire to impress my father and my resentment at being exposed to other people's judgments, particularly my mother's. And worst of all there was my fear of failing.

The film seemed to be vanishing from me. Eighteen locations had up until that time been changed or cut for cost reasons. Over budget and behind schedule, there was a very real possibility of the production guarantor stepping in and taking over. John was attempting to hold down costs. His main worry was that the film might never be finished, mine that it might not be worth finishing. I was on top of a tower when I saw him guiding a woman visitor around the set. I had just learnt that he had slashed another location. I stopped the shooting, descended the tower and stood in front of them. He smiled, but I remained grim-faced and there was an awkward silence before I asked, 'How can you tell when a producer's lying?' He shrugged.

'His lips move,' I said drily. He laughed realising that I had just heard about the latest location cut, while I went back to work smiling, my irritation evaporated for a time.

John and I were arguing like a couple who have lived together for too long, even about the horse. After months of training to jump out of the boat it was struck by a bad case of stage fright on the first night, refusing to jump at all. By four in the morning it still hadn't jumped. I wanted to strangle it or anyone who was responsible for this equine prima donna. Furious memos flew, alterations were made to the boat and the horse returned the next night. This time it performed, no doubt aware it had saved itself from the knacker's yard. But by halfway through the filming the beast was completely bored. Instead of gazing in terror at the submarine, it grazed contentedly on the bottom of the boat. Finally the trainer had to lie under its belly and tickle the horse's legs to make it lift its head. If a take was too long it stepped from the dinghy and swam to shore, often in the middle of a shot. Exhausted by the delays this beast was causing, Marshall refused to come out of his caravan, believing we would not be ready when we said we would. He finally emerged with great reluctance, only to find that the horse had meanwhile grown agitated waiting and had been rowed ashore to calm down.

Then it seemed we were ready to shoot. We were out on this little smelly pond, circling each other in two boats. One of them had a camera mounted on a boom, the

other held Marshall and the horse. The motor on my tiny leaking rubber dinghy broke down and the water proved too deep for the frogman to manoeuvre it easily. Steering with a broken paddle in one hand and a megaphone in the other, I was simultaneously bargaining for overtime on a waterlogged walkie-talkie. Meanwhile Marshall was frantically trying to row his large, leaky, clinker-built boat with the horse in it. The rowlock broke, was fixed, then broke again. Marshall, a normally controlled man, broke too, erupting and shouting, demanding to be rowed ashore. Back on land I slipped in the mud and sprawled, like some comedian pratfalling, face first. I'd had enough. I threw the megaphone against a tree. Not to be outdone, Marshall stormed to his cabin.

A week later I watched from the top of the submarine as the last of the crew packed and drove off into the night. It was then I realised that the conning tower's ladder had been removed, *perhaps* by accident. While I waited for someone to remember and return, I saw myself stranded on top of the conning tower drifting slowly out on an imaginary sea until, as a disappearing speck on the horizon, I became solitary master of my wooden submarine.

By this stage three of my department heads had fallen ill, as had two of the main actors. Perhaps the grimness of the medieval story I was telling was pursuing us into the real world; I knew it was affecting Bruce. Fixing me with those peculiarly piercing eyes, he talked of alchemy, the fire and the blackening. He called the film crew a little band of brothers, a medieval craft guild who were signing their apprenticeship in blood. He saw me as an alchemist, saying with solemn intensity, 'All the alchemists courted madness or death. They risked injury and poisoning, shut out of the light, subjected to huge temperature variations and horrible stinks. They were dark and eccentric and unless they gave up their egos, they were condemned.'

Playing Connor took Bruce to the edge of some part of himself, and became a confrontation with his own fear of failure. 'I feel I am dying,' he whispered, 'until the final moments of the take, and then I come alive. But afterwards I can't imagine how I will ever get through the rest of the film.' Nursing a bruised, possibly fractured rib made his moods even darker, but what made visiting him dispiriting was his conviction that my concern wasn't genuine, that someone had prompted me to see him.

This didn't help my developing siege mentality. I was beginning to sense hostility among some of the crew and I began to feel increasingly separate from them. I knew that my slowness and lack of organisation was responsible for some of the problems, but I felt the real cause of this difficulty was my tendency to direct in a monosyllabic and preoccupied manner.

I was starting to see myself through the eyes of those around me, and I felt uncomfortable at what I recognised. Like my Jewish aunt I was focused totally on my work, unable or unwilling to notice the effect I had on those I worked with. Those who gave the most naturally felt the most neglected and it seemed as though I was interested in them only when they were useful to me. Yet despite this I felt that it came down to shortage of money and lack of time, and with ill-health we were all feeling the strain.

My only option seemed to be to bail the film out with my own money — something John was reluctant to agree to, having already put a part of his own fee on the line. He warned: 'You'll grow old, bitter and twisted waiting for any return.' And so I did.

But time had run out. The main shoot was over and we were missing important sections. I found myself angry with everyone, and as the circle of anger grew tighter I became angry at myself for being angry. It seemed as if it was all disintegrating. Bruce headed for the bush several hundred miles away from our pickup shots, forgetting to leave a forwarding address. Exhausted and no doubt feeling much older than his years,

John left to attend to other projects in Australia. Despite the testiness of our relationship during the shoot, he had stuck by me through all the difficulties and I was sorry to see him go. I stayed on, feeling shrunken and incredibly ancient, to try and finish off with a cameraman and an assistant.

There were no long goodbyes, just the exhausted drifting away. It was Glenys who wanted a fiery ending. As our witch she was eager to get her revenge on the cumbersome wardrobe she'd washed and scrubbed, wanting to cast out the demons within the fibres. She built a fire and with a wild gleam in her eye, started throwing costumes onto the pyre, as she led everyone in a dance around the blaze. But it became a slow dance, for she had forgotten that all the costumes had been coated with a fire retardant. The exorcism finally needed a cocktail of alcohol and petroleum to fire through the many layers of rough weave and weariness.

A desolate handful of survivors stayed on to finish the filming. The sets that had made the dream real lay around us in broken bits. It was as if we were abandoned in a gradually vanishing world. One day I motioned to a rowing boat we needed to use, only to discover it had gone. The final section was shot just ahead of the bulldozer tearing down the sets in an empty production shed, with one apple box, one actor and a camera.

Following my dream, like Griffin had followed his, had burnt us all out. I was in Australia editing when the second unit managed to get the one sequence I had wanted but believed was too hard to do. They were lowered into a cavern over 300 feet underground to film a flaming torch dropping, end over end, through the earth. After their first attempt was rained out, the second was aborted when the cameraman's Arriflex plummeted into an underground river and imploded in its case. Muddy and exhausted, they took more than three hours to haul themselves out of the cavern before travelling back to Auckland. But the next day they were back with another camera, and this time they got the shot.

Somehow all the fragments had come together. When any of the crew of *Navigator* survivors met in the following months, there was a new humour among us, which was helped when the film began to do well. Sitting in a coffee bar in Cannes, Bruce told me he hadn't thought he would get through the shoot. 'I felt such futility, I thought I wasn't strong enough, I wasn't heroic. But two weeks after the filming was done, I knew I felt stronger. Months later you wake up and feel . . . you feel you have courage.'

New Zealand . . . bringing this film back to my home as a success mattered more to me than I thought it would when I left, angry and embittered. John and I had left the country at our lowest ebb, and returned to make the film in lean times. The meaning of the gauntlet, the blindfold and the spire was clear now and they no longer bothered me. I was free of *The Navigator*, and in some ways reconciled towards my home. I was free to leave. Finally I understood that the face behind the blindfold had always been my own, as I tried to envisage the film, and make that vision a reality.

Sitting on my Sydney veranda on a hot afternoon, I remember how as a child I'd watched the sun redden and the sky turn black with smoke from Australian bushfires 1400 miles away. Little wonder then that to this child's eye Australia would always seem like flame to a moth. I idly turn over the matchbox I am holding, and there to my surprise read instructions on how to survive in a bushfire. Where else could you light a match and read of its destructive force a millionfold? But here in this land of brilliant, piercing light I am still unable to shake myself free of my homeland.

The pieces are becoming clearer to me; the old Maori kuia in the forest and the pioneer farmer with his blowtorch, the girl coming of age in *Vigil*, the miner's boy in *The Navigator*, my Jewish aunt and Puhi, and me, sitting here on this Australian veranda. It is the country and the family and the people I come from that give my stories shape. And that I cannot escape.

Before me I half expect to see an old figure in black, leaning on her staff as she trudges on, and before she vanishes into the haze, I hope she turns around and beckons me.

It is time to take new bearings for there is a map in her kit and its paths are many. But though I know I can read it now, I'm still not sure I can find my way.

CONTRIBUTORS

VINCENT WARD is currently working on a project called *Map of the Human Heart*. And was last seen looking for locations in the Arctic.

ALISON CARTER works when she has to as a writer, journalist and researcher. She grew up in small-town New Zealand, made a brief foray to Australia and then left this part of the world in the 1960s for Britain. During her 12 years in Scotland she worked as a student, waitress, community worker, journalist, video-maker and theatrical manager before returning to New Zealand in 1980 to a post as a television journalist. Now she's a trans-Tasman resident who lives out of 57 boxes and is accompanied on her travels by her partner and Winnie the dog.

GEOFF CHAPPLE is an author and scriptwriter. His books include *Rewi Alley of China, 1981: The Tour* and *South*. He has written or co-written three feature film scripts, including *The Navigator*, also television dramas, and radio plays. His interest in things medieval began during an extended trip to one of the most remote areas of China, Gansu Province, in 1979. There, much of the agriculture and village organisation remained bound to the distant past.

Geoff lives in Devonport, Auckland, with his wife Miriam, their children Polly, Irene and Amos, a dog, cat and a chook.

LOUIS NOWRA is an author and playwright who lives in Australia. He met Vincent Ward in a Kings Cross coffee bar. He hasn't been back to the coffee bar since.

GEOFFREY SHORT was born in Hamilton in the same year television arrived in New Zealand, and sees himself very much as part of the TV generation. He studied Fine Arts at Auckland University, majoring in photography, and his early work as an exhibiting artist centred on social documentary and portraiture. More recently the emphasis in his work has shifted to explore human relationships and the urban landscape, through large multiple-image pieces. Currently he is working as a freelance photographer.

MILES HARGEST grew up in rural Southland, and was drawn to photography as a way of examining the cultural comparisons and conflicts he observed travelling in South-east Asia. Returning to New Zealand he was stills photographer (and sometimes cook) on *In Spring One Plants Alone,* and went on to work on *Vigil.* In his earlier work, a keen eye for satire revealed social polarisations most New Zealanders are reluctant to admit exist. His present photographs symbolically reinforce humanity's relationship with the planet and the contemporary environmental crisis. Currently living in Auckland, he works wherever the eye alights.

CREWS

Many people assisted with the making of these films. Limitations of space allow
us to list key contributors only.

IN SPRING ONE PLANTS ALONE
(1981)

Principal Photography Alun Bollinger

Additional Photography Leon Narbey, Vincent Ward

Miles Hargest, Alistair Barry

Editor Christine Lancaster

Sound Steven Upston

Stills Photography Miles Hargest

Producer/Director Vincent Ward

VIGIL
(1984)

Toss Fiona Kay

Elisabeth Penelope Stewart

Hunter Frank Whitten

Grandfather Bill Kerr

Director Vincent Ward

Producer John Maynard

Screenplay Graeme Tetley

Vincent Ward

Director of Photography Alun Bollinger

Production Designer Kai Hawkins

Editor Simon Reece

Costume Designer Glenys Jackson

Music Jack Body

Stills Photography Miles Hargest

THE NAVIGATOR — A MEDIEVAL ODYSSEY
(1988)

Griffin Hamish McFarlane

Connor Bruce Lyons

Arno Chris Haywood

Searle Marshall Napier

Ulf Noel Appleby

Martin Paul Livingston

Linnet Sarah Peirse

Director Vincent Ward

Producer John Maynard

Screenplay Kely Lyons

Geoff Chapple

Vincent Ward

Director of Photography Geoffrey Simpson

Production Designer Sally Campbell

Costume Designer Glenys Jackson

Conceptual Designer Michael Worrall

Editor John Scott

Music Davood Tabrizi

Stills Photography Geoffrey Short

Page 92: detail from Hell Panel, 'The Garden of Earthly Delights', Hieronymous Bosch, 1504. Copyright © Museo del Prado, Madrid. All rights reserved. Reproduction of the image, or any part thereof, is prohibited.

Page 94: detail from 'The Temptation of Saint Anthony', Hieronymous Bosch, *c.* 1495. Copyright © Museo del Prado, Madrid. All rights reserved. Reproduction of the image, or any part thereof, is prohibited.

Page 154: detail from 'A View of the Kipdorp Poort, Antwerp', Maerten van Cleef the Elder, *c.* 1550.

Page 156: detail from fragment of fresco 'The Triumph of Death', Andrea Orcagna, mid-fourteenth century.

Page 160 and 167 (*left*): from 'Curious Woodcuts of Fanciful and Real Beasts', Konrad Gesner, mid-sixteenth century. Courtesy of Dover Publications Inc., New York.

Page 161: from *Do Gentibus Romae*, Olaus Magnus, 1555. Courtesy of Rosenkilde & Bagger, Copenhagen.

Page 162: from *Leben der Heiligen* (Wintertheil), Voragine, 1471.

Pages 164 and 175: from the *Nuremberg Chronicle*, Scheddel, 1493. Courtesy of Weidenfeld and Nicolson Archives, London.

Page 165: 'Darstellung eines Silberbergwerkes in Kuttenberg', detail from the Kutna Hora gradual (Cod. 15501, fol. 1 verso), *c.*1490. Courtesy of the National Library of Austria, Vienna.

Page 167 (*right*): detail of map of Scandinavia, Olaus Magnus, 1572. Courtesy of Dover Publications Inc., New York.

Page 168 (*top*): detail of woodcut, Michael Wohlgemuth, from the *Schatzbehalter*, Nuremberg, 1491.

Page 168 (*bottom*): woodcut, artist unknown, from *Les Songes Drolatiques de Pantagruel*, Rabelais, 1565.

Page 170: from the Luttrell Psalter, British Museum Manuscripts Collection (ADD 42130, fol. 160.), mid-fourteenth century. Courtesy of the British Library, London.

Page 171: detail from 'Temptation to Avarice' in the *Ars Moriendi*, *c.*1465.

Page 172: 'The Elephant', from a bestiary made in England (MS Bodley 764, fol. 12), mid-thirteenth century. Reproduced by permission of the Bodleian Library, Oxford.

Page 174: 'The Lancashire Witches', from *The Famous Lancashire Witches* (a chapbook), London, 1780.